CW00919870

Sinotecture

New Architecture in China • Neue Architektur in China

▶

SINOTECTURE

NEW ARCHITECTURE IN CHINA • NEUE ARCHITEKTUR IN CHINA

Christian Dubrau

INHALT

CONTENTS

PR CHINA'S MAJOR CITIES

1 URUMQUI
2 LHASA
3 XINING
4 LANZHOU
5 YINCHUAN
6 XI'AN
7 HOHHOT
8 TAIYUAN
9 ZHENGZHOU
10 SHIJIAZHUANG
11 BEIJING
12 HEBEI
13 JINAN
14 DALIAN
15 SHENYANG
16 CHANGCHUN
17 HARBIN
18 SHANGHAI
19 HANGZHOU
20 NANJING
21 HEFEI
22 WUHAN
23 NANCHANG
24 CHANGSHA
25 FUZHOU
26 GUANGZHOU
27 SHENZHEN
28 HONG KONG
29 MACAU
30 HAIKOU
31 NANNING
32 GUIYANG
33 CHONGQING
34 CHENGDU
35 KUNMING

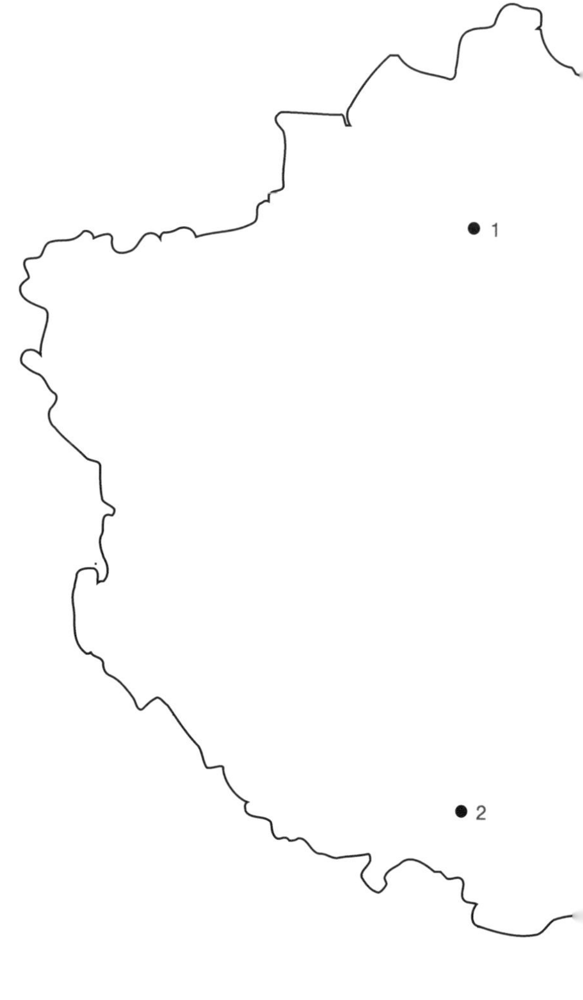

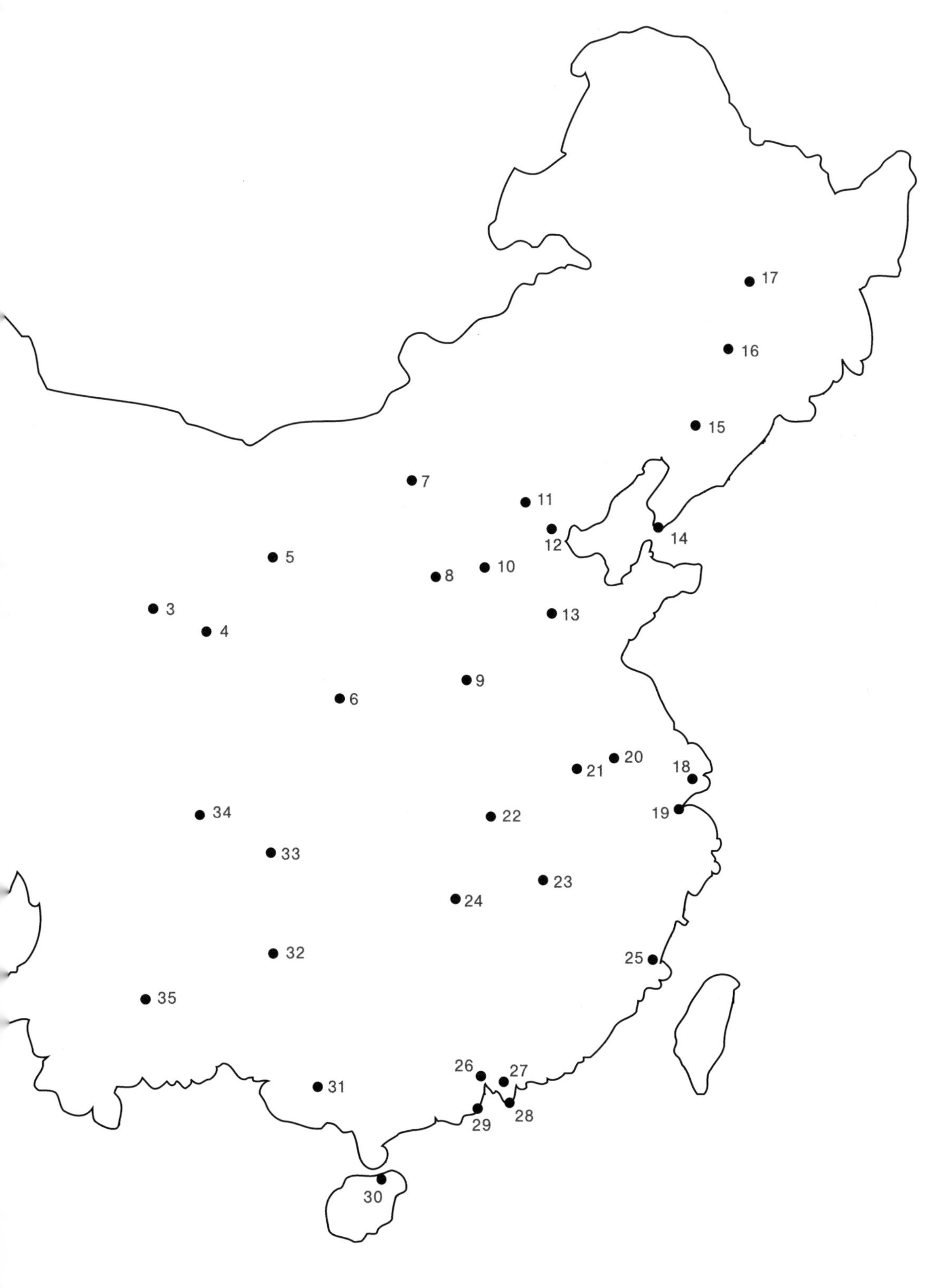

17
16
15
7
11
12
14
5
8
10
3
13
4
9
6
20
21
18
19
34
22
33
23
24
25
32
35
26
27
28
29
31
30

IMAGE ARCHITECTURE

CHINESE ARCHITECTURE SEARCHING FOR IDENTITY AND A SENSE OF BELONGING

HIGH-SPEED-URBANISATION AND HIGH-END-ARCHITECTURE

After many long years of marginal economical and political existence, China is now well on its way towards becoming a superpower. This development is not merely due to the unimaginable tempo of economic growth, but also to the country's growing cultural self-confidence. The opening-up and liberalisation of the country during the last decades of the twentieth century, as well as the ensuing installation of economic zones, ensure uninhibited growth in the core regions. Many foreign investors from abroad who have discovered West China to be a cheap country of production with a good infrastructure or as the world's largest market distribution boost the motor of economic progress. The fact that the world's most populous country has succeeded in winning for itself such global events as the 2008 Olympic Games and the EXPO 2010 seems to confirm all prognoses: no one can afford to ignore China any longer. This meteoric development calls forth immense consequences, above all in China itself.

China has declined into a kind of »high-speed urbanisation.«[1] Of the 1.3 billion people living there,[2] despite immigration limitations already in force, approximately 400 to 500 million will stream into the cities already designated as megacities during the next few years.[3] They want to have a share of the economic boom and drive the demand for living space and workplaces further upwards. There is no end in sight for this trend; it has only just begun.

Shanghai, Beijing and the Pearl River Delta are surely the best-known showplaces of an incredible demolition and construction wave. Growth processes that took place in Europe during the 19th century are now happening in China with a delay, but twice as rapidly and at a considerably larger scale. Parallel to the economic growth, construction projects are being carried out at a breathtaking scale and rapid speed.

For example, one can observe, in Shanghai, how fifty-storey high-rises are built within a brief period of time amongst old two-storey Lilong house settlements, completely changing the area. Only a very few of the original residents remain there.

To relieve the metropolis of Shanghai, nine completely newly-planned satellite cities are being stamped out of the ground within an extremely short period of time – each

[1] *Front cover headline of the German architectural magazine archplus: Chinesischer Hochgeschwindigkeits-urbanismus (Chinese High Speed Urbanism), Vol. 168/2004.*

[2] *The World Factbook, July 2006.*

Anting New Town near Shanghai

one corresponding to a special European model.[4] The city of Anting by the German AS&P Bureau resembles a small German city and is already finished; British, Dutch, Italian and Spanish clone settlements will be following shortly.

Large sections of the river and lake shores are being drained in order to make room for new ideal cities. The water-city Lingang New City (Luchao Harbour City) by the German architectural bureau gmp is especially well known. To the south of Shanghai on the Chinese Sea, a completely new ideal city with an artificial lake at the centre[5] is

[3] *Prof. Wu, Director of the Architecture Faculty of Tongji University Shanghai in the Süddeutsche Zeitung (January 3, 2004, p. 13).*
[4] *Anting, Luodian, Zhujiajiao, Fencheng, Gaoqiao, Fengjing, Pujiang, Zhoupu, Buzhen. (www.sinocities.net).*
[5] *www.gmp-architekten.de*

being built with 74 square kilometres for 800,000 inhabitants, organised in concentric circles and radial axes. But this is not the only settlement on the land drained of water. In the Golf of Hangzhou, the largest newly planned large city is to be built on a surface area of 250 square kilometres. Planned as additional farming land during the 1960s, a master plan has now been prepared for the area by SYNIA (Shangyu New Industrial Area) by the German architects Fink & Jocher. Over 800,000 people will live in the area, which is one thousand times the size of the competitive area of Potsdamer Platz/Leipziger Platz in Berlin.[6]

Until 1978, Beijing was a city of somewhat more than 50 square kilometres with predominantly one and two-storey buildings. Since November 2003, five circular roads with six to ten, in places even fourteen[7] lanes encircle an agglomeration of high-rises on an area of about 600 square kilometres. The sixth circular road is already being built, about 50 kilometres from the city centre. The seventh circular road is already being planned as well, in order to accommodate the ever-growing volume of traffic and property requirements.

Old villages, far away from Beijing 20 years ago, are now encircled by high-rise settlements and are being transformed into affordable and completely overcrowded sleeping and service buildings for hosts of migrant workers or are being successively »renovated.«[8]

The classical city models have long ceased to offer an adequate description of the conurbation of settlement structures in the Far East.[9] As an up-and-coming economical power, China has an uninterrupted craving for admiration and prestige. But also firms, institutions and impending major events require a markedly new, modern »lighthouse« architecture.

Major projects unique in the world are being created for the 2008 Olympic Games in Beijing. The stadium by Swiss architects Herzog & de Meuron called »Bird's Nest« is exemplary for this ambitious development, due to its bizarrely intertwined construction, but so is the swimming stadium by the Australian bureau PTW Architects with load-bearing structure and covering out of airy, blue foam. The headquarters of Chinese television, designed by Rem Koolhaas and Ole Scheeren, is being built alongside approximately 300 new high-rise buildings in the new Central business District of Beijing. With its particularly striking form, it is already now considered the trademark of the broadcasting house, which will also organise the broadcast of the Olympic Games. It is no wonder that the construction site of the »Loop,« jutting 230 metres into the sky, receives more attention than any other.[10]

In Shanghai, EXPO 2010 is leading to similar excesses of self-production in architecture. Alongside the representation of economic power in the new »Financial and Business

[6] www.fink-jocher.de

[7] Two times four lanes on the main road. In addition, two times three parallel lanes for close traffic and turning.

[8] Renovation in this case means complete demolition and new construction of residential high-rises or green areas. See also Barbara Münch, Michael Arri: Simultane Realitäten – Urban Villages in Chinas expandierenden Metropolen, in: Gregor Jansen: totalstadt. beijing case. High-Speed Urbanisierung in China, Cologne 2006, p. 188 – 195.

[9] New terms must be invented to describe these phenomena. See here especially Chuihua J. Chung, Jeffrey Inaba, Rem Koolhaas: Great Leap Forward: Harvard Design School Project on the City, Cologne 2001; and Peter G. Rowe: East Asia Modern: Shaping the Contemporary City, London 2005.

Demolition in Shanghai's Sinan Lu

District« and the expression of technological strength in the Shanghai »Science & Technology Museum,«[11] the city has the ambition to demonstrate its pioneering cultural role as well. Whereas concert halls and opera houses are being forced to close in many large European cities, because the communities can only afford one cultural centre, the following have been built in Shanghai in addition to the Opera House by architect Jean Marie Charpentier opened in 1998: the Concert Hall, renovated in 2004 and displaced 60 metres as well as a dozen sites belonging to the next large entertainment complex by the French architect Paul Andreu accommodating 3,300 spectators.[12]

Beijing, Shanghai, Shenzhen and also Guangzhou and Chongqing are planning skyscrapers of record sizes.[13] The 610-metre high Television and Sightseeing Tower in Guangzhou by Arup/Information Based Architecture will probably be completed in 2009. Shanghai and Beijing want to be perceived as »Global Cities« able to compete with metropolises such as New York or London. Within the country, provincial capitals are vying for attention in the power distribution struggle with similar means. They are decorating themselves with completely oversized high-rises, congress centres, concert halls and exhibition halls, in order to at least be able to communicate a touch of grandeur with a newly designed landmark.

China is probably the only country in which projects can be realised within a very short period of time and in enormous dimensions.[14] Even smaller architectural bureaus such as Fink & Jocher of Munich have the chance of realising large projects in China, but of

[10] *See Bauwelt: OMA, Arup und das CCTV, 07/2007.*
[11] *Project by RTKL Associates (2001).*
[12] *Grand opening on December 31, 2004.*
[13] *As of 2007, the highest skyscraper is the »Taipei Financial Centre – Taipei 101« in Taiwan at 508 metres.*
[14] *See Deyan Sudjic: Die Karawane zieht weiter, in: archplus, Vol. 168/2004, p. 30 – 32.*

course only if they accept the conditions in China and can be on the spot quickly and without fuss after nerve-wracking periods of waiting.
Chinese investors put their trust in Western know-how. However, foreign bureaus are usually only allowed to appear as »design« bureaus. Collaboration with a large licensed Chinese planning institute is more or less compulsory. This forced work distribution is due to the dual structure of the Chinese planning system – Chinese bureaus, too, often design only colourful perspectives of buildings. They must leave the execution to one of the institutes which are specialised in money-saving, standardised building.[15] Thus the realisations often do not correspond to the conceptions of the architectural bureaus because the planning institutes replace specially developed solutions with standard details. In this way, filigree steel constructions are sometimes turned into clumsy reinforced concrete blocks. The only possibility of ensuring quality is often to integrate internationally active engineering companies and realisation firms into the project.

IDENTITY PROBLEMS

The architecture of international bureaus is increasingly being confronted by Chinese criticism. The Opera House by Paul Andreu is seen as being too non-Chinese, not adapted to the context of the environment. Moreover, too much steel – a scarce material – has been used, rendering the project more expensive than necessary. Rem Koolhaas has to listen to similar criticism for his CCTV-Tower and Herzog & de Meuron for their Olympic Stadium. Voices in the media are increasing accusing foreign architects of not understanding Chinese culture and of arrogantly ignoring China's needs.
The criticisms have reached their peak in the suspicion that foreign architects have been using China as a playground for their experimental ideas.[16] It has even been discussed whether foreign bureaus should be excluded from certain projects and competitions.

Be that as it may, Chinese design institutes receive commissions for national prestige projects less frequently than do their colleagues from abroad. The well-known name of the internationally known architect is required for such projects, as is his experience with major projects. It is not for nothing that precisely those architects are chosen who have also won the most important international architecture prize – the Pritzker Prize – or who can demonstrate similarly prestigious honours.
China has an identity problem. This is more than clearly verified by the Dutch cities with windmills built by Dutch architectural bureaus, English cities in Tudor style and Italian cities with piazza and canale. But it is the Chinese investors and executive personnel who want to place Schiller and Goethe on market places after the German model.
The fact that criticism is suddenly bringing in the fighting concept of identity and the lack of understanding for Chinese culture, after many years of uninterrupted glorification

[15] *See Eduard Kögel: Zur Lage junger Architekten in China, in: archplus, Vol. 168/2004, p. 71f.*
[16] *e.g. Zhang Hong: Beijing: Architectural Showcase, in: China today 02/2005.*

of foreign architecture, is not surprising. This discussion is closely linked with global processes worldwide. It begins when an increasing globalisation is understood as an attack against societal, cultural values and traditions. For the economical and cultural globalisation creates a homogenising which makes national differences and regional characteristics disappear. This especially has effects on the architecture in China, the new »global player.«

But what does the identity of Chinese society in fact consist of? What are its characteristics, what can it identify with, and how it is differentiated from others? Viewed from the outside through the media or as a tourist, China appears to be a large, unified nation. The Chinese themselves are convinced of this as well. This is the case for various reasons: in the consciousness of the Chinese, their culture is the oldest in the world. Already recorded in 1000 B. C., it apparently goes way back into mythical times. Already in 2205 B. C. the legendary Emperor Yu is supposed to have founded the Xia Dynasty, thus laying the cornerstone for a high culture lasting over 4,000 years. The astonishing thing is the continuity revealed by the development of Chinese culture. Indeed, no other people in the world can be observed to be a unified and clearly demarcated cultural area over such a long period. There is a strong consciousness of the fact that China was always a great culture. The strength of the long common culture holds the Chinese people together, both in the present and the future.

The second reason is the special Chinese form of »early capitalistic communism« which, as an authoritarian system, is able to hold together and control a nation of 1.3 billion people.

The third reason for this strong cohesion is the present-day economic growth. A positive basic mood created at the national level also has a contagious effect on Western nations which desire to participate in this development.

Chinese workers loading a steel beam from truck by hand.

China's greatest desire is to be perceived as a modern state with a long tradition. However, the suggested national homogeneity does not in fact exist. China is not the unified nation that is being completely modernised in a clear continuation of its own traditions. The ruptures are unmistakeable.
The clearest opposition in this is the conflict between tradition and modernism. Throughout the long tradition, there exists a great connectedness to China's own traditions. Many elements of old China – Buddhism, Taoism and Confucianism – still play an important role today in the society. They are considered not only the standard for what is actually Chinese today, but also serve to demarcate against cultural imports from other parts of the world. The result is, necessarily, a point of view orientated on the past. On the other hand, the economic boom and the nation reacting to global mechanisms create the desire for a new China, detached from old, cumbersome traditions. This coexistence of consciousness for tradition and the striving towards a global, post-industrial society must lead to certain rejections.

While the old population is more closely connected with the traditional modes of living, the young generation is increasingly distancing itself from old systems of values and norms. Twenty years ago, problems of everyday life were solved in familial or working communities (so-called Danweis). They can be interpreted as a continuation of the Confucian societal system of order.[17] Now a pampered generation of single children is growing up, marked by a Western-influenced worship of individuality as well as consumerism and MTV culture. Many young people have developed a completely new conception of themselves. They dream of travelling abroad and of an interesting profession in which they can realise themselves. A generation of parents insisting upon the maintenance of traditional societal principles thus encounters a foreign young generation with completely different views and life-goals of their own.

The gap between city and country also belongs to this generational conflict. Shanghai, Beijing and the Pearl River Delta are motors of the »high-speed urbanisation« being perceived all over the world. However, these growth phenomena only apply to the cities on the east coast and Beijing. Small cities such as Suzhou and Shenzhen, located near the metropolises, are still swimming in the tracks of the megacities. Whether this development will reach all of China is highly questionable. Things look completely different in the regions outside the spheres of influence of the special economic zones. Remote cities such as Chongqing – the world's largest city – have a considerably slower growth. Only some major projects of importance to the entire country – dams or factories – are distributed over all of China. The rural regions seem to have been left behind in their development. Almost feudal structures, backwardness and great poverty mark the picture here.

---

[17] *Barbara Münch: Verborgene Kontinuitäten des chinesischen Urbanismus, in: archplus Vol. 168/2004, p. 44 – 49.*

Olympic stadium, the so-called Bird's Nest

Until a short time ago, the tax system obliged each Chinese person to make a large financial contribution to the modernisation of the special economic zones. Rural development was thus slowed down. Large portions of the rural population were brought to the edge of their existence – one of the main reasons for the flight from the country and the large movement of migrant workers streaming into the cities. Now, infrastructural furtherance programmes with names like »Development of Socialistic Villages of the New Type«[18] are supposed to give small cities the possibility of profiting a little bit from the economical upswing.
But this development is making slow progress. The policy cannot eliminate the consequences of a one-sided furtherance of the special economic zones and the neglect of the hinterland all at once. In view of these contrasts, one can hardly speak of a unified Chinese identity.

WESTERN ARCHITECTURE BECOMES CHINESE MODERNISM

The rapidly constructed buildings in a »business district« are especially intended to communicate modernity. The point is the outward effect and image. This is why style and symbols are important design criteria of a building. It is too much to expect of Chinese architecture, however, to produce fitting images with their own specific identity at a high tempo. This is why they are working less on specific concepts than falling back upon standardised patterns from Western countries which are considered modern in China. Western architectural writings are used as models for designs, as are the construction books of the 19th century.[19]

---

[18] Lan Xinzhen: Construction of Socialistic Villages of the New Type, in: Beijing Overview 15/2006.

[19] In China, architecture was pure handicraft until the 19th century. One built according to construction books which showed exactly how the constructional tasks were to be executed. A famous example is the long-valid »Yingzao fashi« (Constructional Norms) by Li Jie from the year 1103 A. D. See also Guo Qinghua: Yingzao Fashi. Twelfth-Century Chinese Building Manual, in: Architectural History: Journal of the Society of Architectural Historians of Great Britain, 41/1998.

Often a building must already be sold before it is completed. Thus it is not execution plans and guiding details which are the most important and decisive results of a planning process, but the rendering of a building – provided with water surfaces, fountains, lighting effects birds or airplanes according to the respective sales arguments. Appropriate fantasy names put together from English or European word-fragments such as »Wonderland,« »Dance Moma,« »Soho,« »Western Paradise« or »Rheinstein« belong to these.[20]

The architecture resulting from this disappears behind its image, heavily laden with meaning. Many struggle for attention with similar means. Striking buildings which are all constructed according to a similar pattern are the result. Not variety and individuality are the goal, but a certain outward effect intended to signalise the feeling of belonging: either to the modern world or to the Chinese nation.

»Exhibition halls« especially belong to the buildings intended to express the new economic power. These buildings are often constructed as steel-glass structures possessing an all-embracing, dynamic shed-roof as a striking sign of recognition. Since the buildings are all very similar, the aim of giving prominence to one of them compared to the others is lost. The halls are often little-used, either due to their remote location in a newly constructed »new district« or »business district,« or due to their inadequate ground-plan configurations. This is not problematical, since the chief aim is representation and not a flexible or intensive utilisation. Photos of the façades decorate local event and information brochures for investors. Moreover, school classes and wedding couples are photographed in front of such buildings. The concept functions very well. An identification of the populace with the symbols of modernism is taking place as long as the desire for distancing from tradition remains.

It does not always have to be modernism, however. Tempo, arbitrariness and lack of imagination lead to all possible manifestations of an almost one-to-one copy of European architecture.

Classical forms or styles of European holiday regions especially produce homey atmospheres in residential buildings. Residential settlements are built which resemble theme parks. Butterfly shapes or musical instruments, Spanish villages or Greek temples cover up the fact that many old residents were previously dispossessed. The new apartments are constructed according to taste in appropriate styles such as Imperial Eclectic Style, European Modern Style or Beyond Vision Style. Desires and dreams have been fulfilled in architecture with sparkling plastic palm trees in the inner courtyards and a resonant name for the development. A temporary sales pavilion which over-stimulates all the senses completes the picture.

[20] Shenzhen Wonderland Phase IV – Vanke Developer; Dance Moma – Steiner Modern Engineering & Project Management Co., Ltd.; Western Paradise Walk – Longhu Real Estate; Rheinstein – Beijing Rheinstein Equestrian Centre, Ltd.; Jianwai SOHO – SOHO China Ltd.

Xingtiandi quarter in Shanghai with revitalised traditional Lilong houses

THE ROLE OF TRADITIONAL CHINESE ARCHITECTURE

With buildings in which the specifically Chinese element plays an essential role, native architectural history is frequently drawn upon to create images. After all, China can look back upon a 3,000-year history. Nonetheless, attempts at making references all too often produce very conflicting results.

A circular opening as an entrance into the courtyard of an old Chinese courthouse was anchored in Confucian and Taoist teachings. However, the application of such stylistic means in high-rise buildings is usually detached from their original meaning. The era of curved traditional roofs indiscriminately placed everywhere on new buildings is not yet over.

Still, the superficial appropriation of traditional stylistic means convinces people in China that a building is Chinese and corresponds to their culture. The architecture with floating metal roofs and steel-glass façades is considered foreign – even though it amounts to the majority of building activity in China. People are aware that this form of architecture is imported. It is nevertheless astonishing that the symbols of ancient China are still understood. Chinese symbols, including certain colours, forms and symbols are recognised and correctly interpreted. Only the old rules and prohibitions are neglected there. In ancient China, only the Emperor was allowed to possess yellow roofs. Today there are many buildings in Beijing with yellow roofs because they stand for luck, power and wisdom. This makes it clear that the content of the symbols plays a role, but that the meaning is gradually being lost. Still, certain traditions are proving to be very strong, especially if they are concerned with promising meanings. Thus, white is still considered a colour of mourning; triangular structures or divisions into seven elements are not popular.

Entire street-blocks, quarters or entire cities are being rebuilt in traditional methods of construction, especially in areas with the emphasis on tourism. Parks are completed with classical pavilion architecture and pagodas, temples and palaces are newly constructed.
Since Shanghai no longer has a historical centre, a new old centre is being built round the only surviving historical tea-house. The city wall of Xi'an has not been completely preserved. A new construction now replaces the missing parts. In Kaifeng, too, the capital of the Song Dynasty, it is important to transmit a particularly traditional Chinese image. To achieve this, work was begun early on a new shopping centre in traditional style leading to the old dragon temple. Preserved courthouse estates had to be torn down to make room for the adjoining extension, however.
In the old part of Beijing, too, old courthouse estates are being torn down, despite the protests[21] of dispossessed residents, and replaced by new luxury court houses. The court house is reduced to a principle of design. The marketing of the property is optimised. What remains are grey walls painted red. The original population is herded into newly constructed developments far away from Beijing or insufficiently recompensed.[22]
One has the impression that the Chinese have developed a love for their old ancient architecture, which fascinates them in similar way to the way it fascinates Western tourists – it is exotic. The transfigured glance back towards the past is following the over-fulfilled desire for modernisation. Nevertheless, indiscriminate copies massively hinder the further development their own traditions.
The urban quarter of Xingtiandi in Shanghai, reformed by the American architects Benjamin Wood and Carlos Zapata, is the first project in which an old urban quarter with traditional Lilong houses has been revitalised. Compared to other projects, this is a great advance. However, the original and unique character of the Lilong social network has not been

[21] Protests are almost always in vain. Well-known artists such as Wei Wei and Zhang Dali regularly call attention to the problem. So far, only the case of a Kung Fu master from Chongqing is known in which he succeeded in forcing a better compensation. See Kirstin Wenk: Ein Paar kämpft um sein Haus – und wird berühmt, in: Die Welt, March 25, 2007, and by the same author: Entschädigung für Protestpaar. Haus in Chongqing abgerissen, in: Die Welt, April 4, 2007. See also contributions by Zhang Jie, Wang Jun and Ou Ning in: Gregor Jansen: totalstadt. beijing case, Cologne 2006.
[22] See also Philippe Pataud Célérier: Speculation in Shanghai, in: Le Monde Diplomatique, 1/2007.

Jin Mao tower in Shanghai, for years the world's tallest skyscraper (photograph taken in 2003)

preserved here. Only parts of the building structure and façades have proven themselves worthy of preservation. Today, this quarter is one of the most popular areas of the metropolis for going out, with its international café chains, designer bars and luxury restaurants. Because of its success, this form of dealing with old city structures has already found some imitators. An example is the »Bridge 8« area in the immediate vicinity of the creative commercial area, in which offices, shops, and showrooms were renovated.

Almost without exception, it is architecture created before 1911 which is considered worthy of preservation and realisable. One has the impression that the original Chinese elements in the consciousness of the Chinese ended with the Revolution. The longing and desire for continuity simply blots out the painful rupture of the past decades.
At any rate, one has been able to observe for some time that old industrial facilities have been converted into galleries and arts courtyards. The arts quarter »Machine Factory 798« has had a pioneering role in this. The free artistic scene in Beijing successfully occupied the industrial halls built in 1956 by GDR engineers and is making use of the »industry chic« for the staging of alternative projects. Commercial concepts follow the factory aesthetic trend – in the northern city-centre of Shanghai, a factory built in 1928 was converted into an event and leisure mile called »The New Factories.« Similar plans are being realised in Chongqing and Hangzhou. A considerably more sensitive approach to old building substance can be seen, independent of specific stylistic directions.

ECOLOGY AS AN IMAGE

A new form of energy-saving ecological architecture is developing in China independently from larger trends. Their goals are still aimed high, whereas their realisation continues to be slow. But this will continue to find greater distribution with the help of state subsidies at the highest level, opening up a new field of activity in Chinese architecture.
The ecological aspect can no longer be eliminated from European architecture. Strict environmental regulations have meanwhile found their way into all European building laws. This is also being perceived in the Kingdom of the Centre – ecological architecture serves as an indicator of modernity. Environment-friendly technologies are being used in order to present a modern image to the world. This can be very clearly seen in the plans for EXPO 2010.

A cooperation initiative was founded between Hamburg and Shanghai for these preparations in order to encourage energy-saving and ecological building. Ecobuild 2006 introduced nine new building projects which reduced energy consumption by 75 % compared to that of the usual buildings. Projects such as the Pujiang Intelligence Valley, a highly efficient office building with 12,000 square metres of usable area, are frequently visited display objects which will surely find imitators.[23]

[23] *www.green-shanghai.com*

Machine Factory 798

The major project within the framework of EXPO 2010 in Shanghai, under the motto »Better City, Better Life,« is the new satellite city of Dongtan Eco City.

New ecological concepts are not necessarily combined with each other here, but they are extremely efficient. Limited building heights, greenery on the roofs, and traffic-free zones are the image presented. The city is supplied exclusively by renewable energy forms (wind power, photo-voltaics, bio-masses). Several water reprocessing plants and rubbish recycling plants complete the concept. The city is intended to exceed the environmental standards of the Western world by far. The Olympic Games in Beijing, too, have similar criteria anchored in their advanced goals: they are to be »Green Games.«[24] For example, the goal has been set to have the sky appear »blue« at least 230 days per year; this is to be achieved by considerably reducing pollution. The city has an environment-friendly image for at three decisive weeks during which guests are there from all over the world. This is being carried out in the Chinese manner with all available means.

[24] *http://en.beijing2008.cn*

Large operations are being moved or closed, five new underground lines are being built[25] and over 800 hectares of green areas laid out in the inner city of Beijing.[26] Reforestation programmes for over 10,700 hectares of forest are being carried out[27] and comprehensive traffic bans issued at decisive moments. The roofs are also being provided with greenery on a large scale, in order to make a more environment-friendly impression from above, especially in the approach corridor of the airport. Ecological strategies are not taken due to an ecological consciousness, but because of the hypermodern, Western image that they embody.

A second aspect of the subject of ecology is increasingly gaining in importance, since it influences economical interests. The unlimited economical growth is being threatened because energy resources are limited and the disadvantages of environmental pollution are becoming noticeable in some areas. Pollution is growing along with the economy; it has meanwhile become a problem on a national scale. According to the IEA study, China is already environment culprit number two, measured by the amount of CO_2 production, and will overtake the USA in 2010.[28]
The application of energy-saving technologies is necessary in order to continue growing at the same tempo. The 11th five-year plan (2006 – 2010) has the goal of a 20-percent reduction of energy consumption. Guidelines and legal regulations are being intensified. Especially in the building trade, energy savings of up to 65% are being required. Costs will be considerably reduced through more environment-friendly heating and cooling systems, as well as resource-saving building materials. One fourth of the present buildings are to be renovated with energy-saving measures.[29] These high goals have by no means been reached, however. To reach them, experienced architects from abroad are being invited to put new »modern« ecological concepts into practice.
Already starting in 2002, AS&P used heat insulation for the buildings in the new city of Anting because this was also a component of a »good German city.« In the residential project MOMA Beijing, the Austrian architectural bureau Baumschlager & Eberle applied current building climate concepts such as concrete core cooling and controlled living-space ventilation, attaining a standard which even exceeded European norms.[30]
The planning of the Hypergreen-Tower in Shanghai by Jacques Ferrier in cooperation with the Lafarge-Group plans that 70 percent of the project's own energy requirements are to be self-produced through geothermics, 10 wind power facilities and 3,000 square metres of photovoltaic panels. Controlled living-space ventilation, natural ventilation and dual-layered façades will additionally reduce energy requirements.[31]
Similar concepts are being applied at Pearl River Tower – by the American bureau SOM in Guangzhou. After its completion in 2009, it will be probably the first zero-en-

[25] *Lines 4, 5, 10, Airport-Line and Olympic-Line.*
[26] *For the most part through »renovation« (demolition) of former villages. See Barbara Münch, Michael Arri: Simultane Realitäten – Urban Villages in Chinas expandierenden Metropolen, in: Gregor Jansen: totalstadt. beijing case, Cologne 2006, p. 188 – 195.*
[27] *About the size of the city of Kassel, Germany.*
[28] *See also Agnès Sinai: Late Awakening in the Greenhouse China, in: Le Monde Diplomatique 1/2007.*

Residential buildings next to Dalian International Airport

ergy skyscraper in the world. Going beyond the well-established climatic and energy concepts,[32] a specially formed façade directs wind streams on the skyscraper surface into two wind-channels, where they are transformed into energy by turbines. Fuel cells, humidity condensors and heat exchangers round off the concept and additional serve to gain fresh water.[33]

An important aspect in this project is that the ecological characteristics are clearly seen in them. No clay huts are being reservedly built in the second row. These must be strikingly large projects which will astonish the entire world.

China is on the way towards becoming the world's greatest environmental culprit due to the economic growth, lack of environmental protection regulations and ecologically fatal projects such as the Three-Gorge Dam criticised all over the world. On the other hand, radical ecological concepts are being realised in dimensions which are not possible elsewhere. Despite all China's efforts at showing itself to be a country of ecological superlatives, however, such display projects seem to be a questionable creation of image in view of the disastrous exploitation of nature and people's health.

CHINA'S YOUNG ARCHITECTS

An important component of the current architectural scene is the no longer unimportant national avant-garde movement. The very frequently image-laden, inconsiderate approach of the recent past has produced a counter-movement which is producing good architecture far removed from the mainstream of European models. A young generation of Chinese architects, most of who studied abroad, is returning to China and design-

[29] *Energy Efficiency, a Leitmotif for the 11th Five-Year Plan, in: Infobrief China 2006 (www.china.ahk.de).*

[30] *www.minergie.ch/download/Referat_Eberle.pdf*

[31] *www.lafarge.com*

[32] *Two-leaf cavity wall, anti-sun glass and a shading arrangement, concrete core cooling and photovoltaics.*

[33] *Zentralverband Sanitär Heizung Klima (ed.): Energie und Architecture, Berlin 2007.*

ing buildings in their own offices independently of large design institutes. Functionality and a very subtle approach to regional characteristics mark this architecture. Through skilled and pragmatic tactics with constraints, concepts are being developed with a greater awareness of materials, space, landscape and social structures. Thus already existing buildings are incorporated, regional technologies and spatial concepts are applied; local materials are used and combined with the language of contemporary architecture. The counter-movement is not limited to the three cities of Shanghai, Beijing and Hong Kong. It is architecture of the niche. Smaller projects with much leeway are in the foreground. These architects are successful where people can act with self-determination without having to fulfil large national interests. The building owners are the new elite being formed with individual needs. They give small studios without »1st-Class Registration«[34] the possibility of developing and applying clear design ideas of their own without having to overload their buildings with too many meanings. In contrast to customary practice, building plans are accompanied from beginning to end so that the ideas are really applied and with quality.

The trailblazers of the avant-garde – Ma Qingyun, LIU Jiakun, Ai Wei Wie, Zhang Lei and Wang Shu have begun, in small bureaus, to realise villas, private houses, but also restaurants and shops with high standards in design and application.[35] For example, Ma Qingyun began his independent building activity in China with the house for his father in Lantian. Ai Wei Wie's first architectural project was his own house, built in a 60-day performance. Villas for artists then followed. One of the most outstanding and unusual projects of the new avant-garde is the small Liuyeyuan Museum for Buddhist Sculptures by LIU Jiakun (Atelier Feichang). It was commissioned by a private owner in Xinmin, a small village near Chengdu. Despite the adaptation to local building techniques and materials such as concrete, the building contrasts with its trivial environment through its archaic architectural language. The visitor arrives at the centre of the artificial stone through a small opening on a bridge leading over a lotus pond in a bamboo grove. The ingenious path is continued on the inside, directing the visitor along the exhibition pieces and repeatedly allowing for focussed views onto the landscape and the interior. The element of water regains its traditionally important architectural significance.

Alongside private building owners, universities have also been attempting to establish their image on a qualitatively high level through high-quality architecture for the past few years. An architectural language is necessary which will find international recognition through its conceptual approach and a clearly structured application.

One of the first showcase projects is the Library of Wenzheng College, Suzhou, by the Amateur Architecture Studio (Wang Shu): a crossroads of Chinese pavilion architecture

[34] In order to obtain commissions or realisation plans and building accompanying, a »1st-Class Registration« is required. This system was introduced during the course of the privatisation of the planning system during the 1990s. Even if the number of registrations is increasing, it is still difficult to obtain this licence. See also Eduard Kögel: Zur Lage junger Architekten in China, in: archplus, Vol. 168/2004, p. 71.

[35] See Eduard Kögel: Made in China. Neue chinesische Architektur, Munich 2005.

Liuyeyuan Museum for Buddhist Sculptures, Xinmin

with white modernism. The result is a building with two-storey reading halls stacked up over each other, directed towards the water through large glass surfaces. A middle part with an entrance area pushes through the main structure, revealing a detached reading pavilion approaching the water. The simple form and a logical arrangement support the clarity and precision of the architectural language.

In a similarly well thought-out way, MADA s.p.a.m. has designed the campus of Zhejiang University in Ningbo, Zhang Lei the building of Nanjing University and the Atelier Deshaus the campus of the Institute of Technology in Dongguan.[36] The Atelier Z+ (Zhang Bin, Zhou Wei) has created the basis for a good education for future architects with the new building of the Architecture Faculty at Tongji University in Shanghai.

New bureaus are created each month with confident, pithy and ambiguous names such as Urbanus, Standardarchitecture and Atelier 100s+1 which are attempting to produce architecture in similar ways.
The pioneers of the new architecture are meanwhile known throughout the world, have been represented at several international exhibitions and receive major commissions which, until recently, were granted exclusively to established design institutes or international architectural bureaus. The Bureau MADA s.p.a.m. (Ma Qingyun), for example, has realised, alongside projects in Wuxi, Longyang, Xi'an und Qingpu several major projects simultaneously in Ningbo. Tianyi Square gives the city a new centre, at the same time creating a high-quality public space, the likes of which China has never had before. The project also attempts to combine the small details of the old city with

[36] *Institute for Electro-Technology, Institute for the Free Arts and Institute for Computer Sciences.*

the scale of a newly grown metropolis. The residential, commercial and entertainment quarter, »Y-Town,« north of the centre, combines historical building substance with new architecture based upon traditional forms in a former waterfront area. In places, however, it contrasts with the historical elements through intentionally placed single elements. One of these modern buildings is the Museum for City Planning. Rooms of different uses and sizes subtly influence the façade structure of differently coloured glass building-blocks, so that inner structures are also hinted at on the exterior.[37]

The influences of current Western architecture are unmistakeable in almost all the projects of the new generation. Chinese architects are indeed at work here, but they have often studied abroad and bring a Western approach into their work. Back in their homeland, they attempt to combine these experiences with Chinese traditions and building culture, but increasingly distance themselves from what most Chinese people feel. The long-time collaboration with Rem Koolhaas can be sensed in the diagrammatic-abstract approaches and overlapping layers of MADA s.p.a.m. LIU Jiakun's way of dealing with materials also has a materialistic approach as one otherwise knows from Switzerland. Admittedly, the work of the young »independents« is introducing a quantum leap in quality desired in China's architecture. But the high-quality exposed concrete walls form such an abstract link to Chinese architectural culture that they initially evoke a maximum distance in their foreground clarity. Just as the modernism of the 1920s led a lonely avant-garde life in Europe, there is a danger here that this form of architecture could remain an isolated phenomenon which could be buried in the great mass of trivially image-laden anonymous architecture.

EXPERIMENTAL PRAGMATISM

The great majority of built architecture somehow combines everything with everything, with disregard for concept and meaning. With few exceptions, the result is an overladen architecture, monotonously exciting and eclectically symbolic. It is not without its attractions, but at the same time without any innovative value. Anything that is successful can be copied. Chinese architecture is meanwhile so extensively publicised and the pool of Chinese buildings so large that architects need no longer fall back only upon European architecture. Fewer foreign concepts, more of their own successful concepts form reference points with ever greater frequency. For example, the roof of the Shanghai Opera House is a very popular motif which is often reproduced. And the project »The New Bund« on Shanghai-Pudong once again imitates the successful over-building of the metropolis.

[37] *See Kristin Feireiss, Hans Jürgen Commerell: Ningbo, Metamorphose einer chinesischen Stadt, Berlin 2003.*

Library for Wenzheng College, Suzhou

Especially in residential building, intentional symbolism is being replaced by pure pragmatism. High-rises 200-metres tall stand next to each other, staggered towards the south and jolted towards to north, in bedroom cities with few services, no work and no life. The south side has balconies and living-room windows – calculated by computer programmes which have figured out the amount of sunshine in each room for one's own and the neighbouring building.[38] Floor-plans are used over and over; there are only variations in the selection of colours and a few façade details. The main thing is that the foundation is not missing a canopy and the penthouse is not missing an antenna. Through opulent decorative elements, frames and crowns, the large buildings give the impression of having

[38] The regulation that at least one hour of sunlight must shine in each apartment is at the same time the most important sales argument. Sometimes one suspects that certain designing intentions, such as large openings in the façade, are exclusively due to such regulations.

[39] See Eduard Kögel: Die letzten hundert Jahre: Architektur in China, in: Gregor Jansen: totalstadt. beijing case, Cologne 2006, p. 99 – 123.

more space than they actually have. Many different shapes form merely an agglomerate thrown together out of masses. They build what is effective in the rendering – large roofs, water course with fountains, glaring, shining façades.

The problem of monotony, typical for the 1990s, has been definitively eliminated by the free real estate market.[39] The monotony of white-tiled row houses with green-coloured glazing has been overcome. The different interpretations of the right style lead to different buildings. Thus new high-rises with blue, green or yellow façades alternate with reconstructed temples and city villas in European style – a coexistence of traditional and modern architecture.

If possible, architecture nonetheless remains connected to its context. No skyscrapers will be placed in a park with integrated pavilion architecture. There will be no temple architecture built in a New Business District if it wasn't there before. A holiday settlement is preferably built in Spanish style because it corresponds to the customary idea of holiday-making, and the exhibition halls of the Terracotta Army are resplendent in monumental style. A modern steel-glass construction belongs to a railway station (e. g. Suzhou Railway Station) unless it functions as the gateway to a historically significant city (e. g. Kaifeng railway Station).

The signs used are orientated towards the desired expression: either modernity or awareness of tradition, i. e. Western or Chinese. Thus a society caught between tradition and modernism is looking for the architecture which suits it. The variety of styles and signs is the expression of a differentiated society which has abandoned a closed, collective identity in favour of a plurality of consciousnesses and identifications.

OUTLOOK

The fact that Chinese architecture has meanwhile become internationally noticed and has participated at exhibitions in Berlin,[40] Rotterdam,[41] Paris[42] and Venice[43] is reason for optimism, for this position establishes its substance at home. The architects of the initial avant-garde movement are meanwhile professors at the universities and are educating a new generation of architects.[44] Building owners and developers are increasingly aware that they can attain a competitive advantage through well-conceived and qualitatively high-value buildings and ecological strategies. The courage required in order to arrive at different solutions with inventive experiments has certainly grown. In the area of architecture, China offers the possibility of finding solutions unique in the world by using all its potentials.

[40] Aedes Berlin: TU MU. Junge Architektur aus China, September 21 – October 28, 2001; Aedes Berlin: MADA On Site, February 6 – March 21, 2004 (also in Barcelona, Vienna and Birmingham).
[41] NAI Rotterdam: China Contemporary, June 10 – September 3, 2006.
[42] Centre Pompidou, Paris: What about China?, June 25 – October 13, 2003.

Hong Kong Night View

Property ownership still plays a subsidiary role, so that planning on an untold magnitude is conceivable and realisable. The tempo in the realisation is just as unique as the zest for experimentation. The further opening-up of the country creates more and more free space for private initiatives. Uninterrupted know-how transfer leads to an improvement in quality. With an increasing city-country contrast, as well as foreseeable demographical conflicts, the architecture and city building of China is facing great tasks and challenges. In these conditions, the young generation of architects is equipped with a better understanding of concept and context. Whether or not the future belongs to them on the world building site of China, remains to be seen.

[43] *Contribution of the artists and architect Chang Yung Ho at the Venice Biennale 2005.*
[44] *Chang Yung Ho is Dean of the Graduate Centre for Architecture, University of Beijing. In early 2007 Ma Qingyun will take over a post as Dean of the School of Architecture at the University of Southern California (USC). Wang Lu is Professor at the Tsinghua University Beijing and Editor-in-Chief of the »World Architecture Magazine«.*

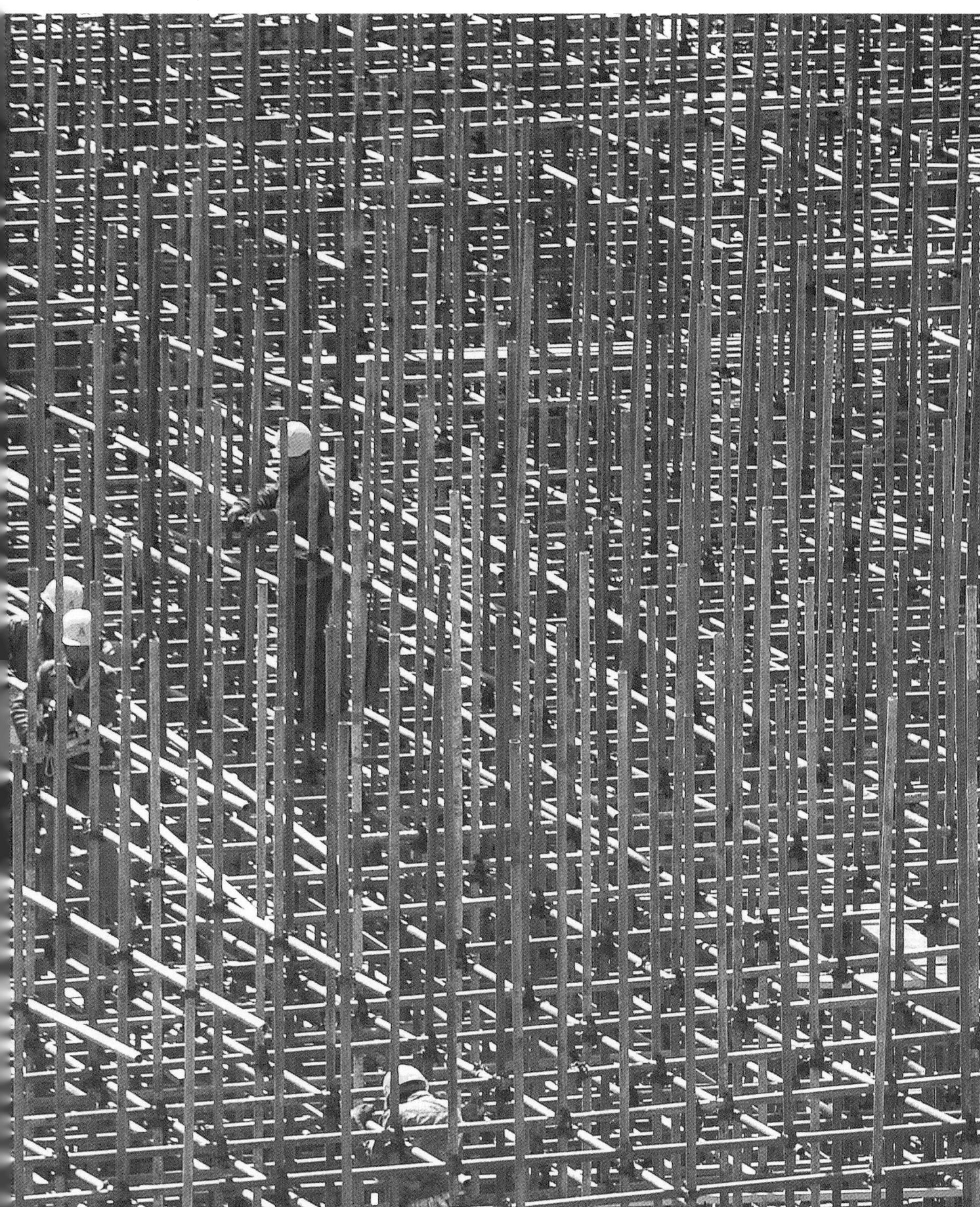

现
代
城
Stadtstaat
CITY-STATES OF THE SABAOTH
盛邦德
喷绘 0755-83320644

公司李欢青年突击队朱景明青年突击队李文标青年突击队
中冶监理

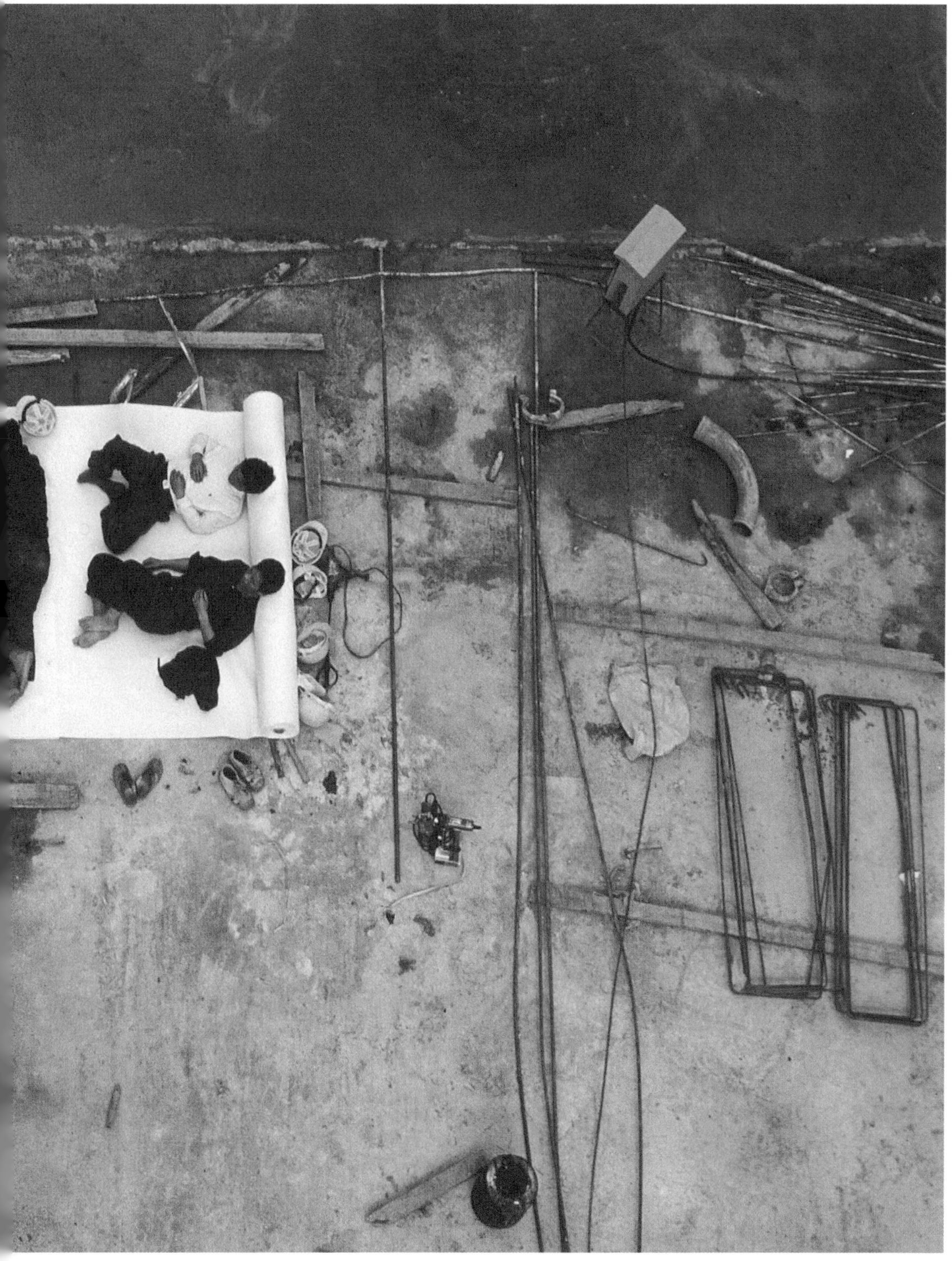

南方证券

FOODIES

八大欢乐迎

ATELIER DESHAUS

▼

Liu Yichun
Zhuang Shen
Chen Yifeng

www.deshaus.com

This studio had its beginnings in a small architecture firm founded in 2001 by three graduates of Tongji University. The young architects had already won a number of prizes for their designs and taken part in significant expositions at home and abroad. Foremost among the architects' considerations are the context in which a given project is set and their plans take account not only of the history of the location but also of factors such as sun, wind, noise and climate. These influence the choice of materials, colour and shape. The planners see their roots as firmly anchored in the western architecture of the modern age.

Das Studio ging aus einem kleinen Architekturbüro hervor, das im Jahr 2001 von drei Absolventen der Universität Tongji gegründet wurde. Die jungen Architekten hatten mit ihren Entwürfen bereits einige Preise gewonnen und an wichtigen Ausstellungen im In- und Ausland teilgenommen. Bei ihren Projekten nehmen die Architekten viel Rücksicht auf den jeweiligen Kontext und beziehen neben der Geschichte des Ortes auch solche Faktoren wie Sonne, Wind, Geräusche und Klima in die Planung ein. Danach richtet sich die Wahl der Materialien, Farben und Formen. Ihre architektonischen Wurzeln sehen die Planer ganz klar in der westlich geprägten Moderne.

▲
Project Computer Department Building, Dongguan University of Technology | **Location** Songshan Lake New Town, Dongguan, Guangdong Province | **Purpose** education | **Area** 15,310 m² | **Completion** 05.2004 | **Architect** Zhuang Shen (in charge)

▶
Project Zhangjiang High-tech Park Service Center | **Location** Songtao road, Zhangjiang High-tech Park, Shanghai
Purpose offices | **Area** 35,000 m² | **Completion** 2004 | **Architect** Atelier Deshaus (preliminary architectural design)
Associate AS&P GmbH and East China Architectural Design & Research Institute

Project Xiayu Nursery School, Qingpu New Town
Location New Town of Qingpu District, Shanghai
Purpose education
Area 6,500 m²
Completion 11.2004
Architect Chen Yifeng (in charge)

Playground, various views
Site plan
Verschiedene Ansichten
Lageplan

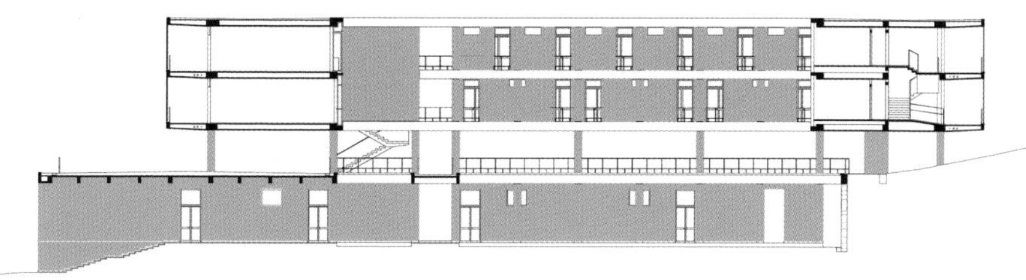

▲ ▶
Project Liberal Arts Building
Location Songshan Lake New Town, Dongguan, Guangdong Province
Purpose education
Area 9,150 m^2
Completion 05.2004
Architect Chen Yifeng (in charge)

◀
Project Electronics Department Building, Dongguan University of Technology
Location Songshan Lake New Town, Dongguan, Guangdong Province
Purpose education
Area 20,860 m^2
Design/Completion 08.2004
Architect Liu Yichun (in charge)

UNIVERSAL ARCHITECTURE STUDIO

Hua Li

Yang Hongsheng

▶ www.uas-arch.com

This company, established in 2003, operates at the interface between academic research and architectural practice. The owners see themselves as purveyors of formal innovation and see architecture not simply as a means to an end but also as a medium for a lifestyle that represents a quite new cultural phenomenon in China. The creation of new buildings and spaces has led to the emergence of new spheres of human self-realisation – in towns, streets and buildings alike. Architecture is to a large extent the product of dialogue involving a location, a period, the people and their needs. Chinese architecture is peculiar in that it springs from the tension between a collective culture handed down through the generations and the burgeoning age of western individualism as determined by capitalist market forces.

Das 2003 gegründete Büro arbeitet an der Schnittstelle von akademischer Forschung und architektonischer Praxis. Die Inhaber verstehen sich als Vermittler formaler Innovation und begreifen Architektur nicht nur als Mittel zum Zweck, sondern als Medium eines Lifestyle, der in dieser Form ein neues kulturelles Phänomen in China ist. Mit der Schaffung neuer Räume werden auch neue Sphären der menschlichen Selbstverwirklichung kreiert – in Städten ebenso wie auf Straßen oder in Gebäuden. Architektur entsteht in einem Dialog zwischen dem Ort, der Zeit, den Menschen und ihren Bedürfnissen. Das Besondere an der chinesischen Architektur beruht auf dem Spannungsverhältnis zwischen einer tradierten kollektiven Kultur und dem anbrechenden Zeitalter eines westlichen Individualismus unter den Bedingungen eines kapitalistischen Marktes.

▲ ▶ ▼

Project Jingya Xicuilu Ocean Entertainment Center, Beijing
Location Xicuilu road, Beijing | **Purpose** leisure | **Area** 16,000 m² | **Design/Completion** 2003/2005
Designteam: Architectural Hua Li, Yang Hongsheng, Li Wen, Zhang Chong | **Structural** Ge Jiaqi **MEP** Li Jianjun, Pan Jun, Yang Haizhong

▲▲
◀▲
Construction site
Façade
3-D animation
Section
Baustelle
Fassade
Drei-D-Animation
Schnitt

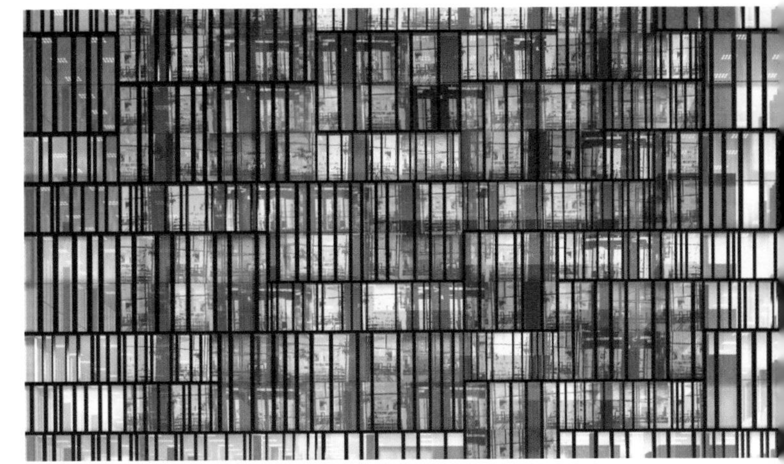

◀ ▲ ▼
Project Zhonglian Office Complex, (competition, first prize) Beijing, 2005
Location Zhichun road & South Tsinghua road, Haidian District, Beijing
Purpose offices
Area 32,000 m^2
Design/Completion 2005/2006

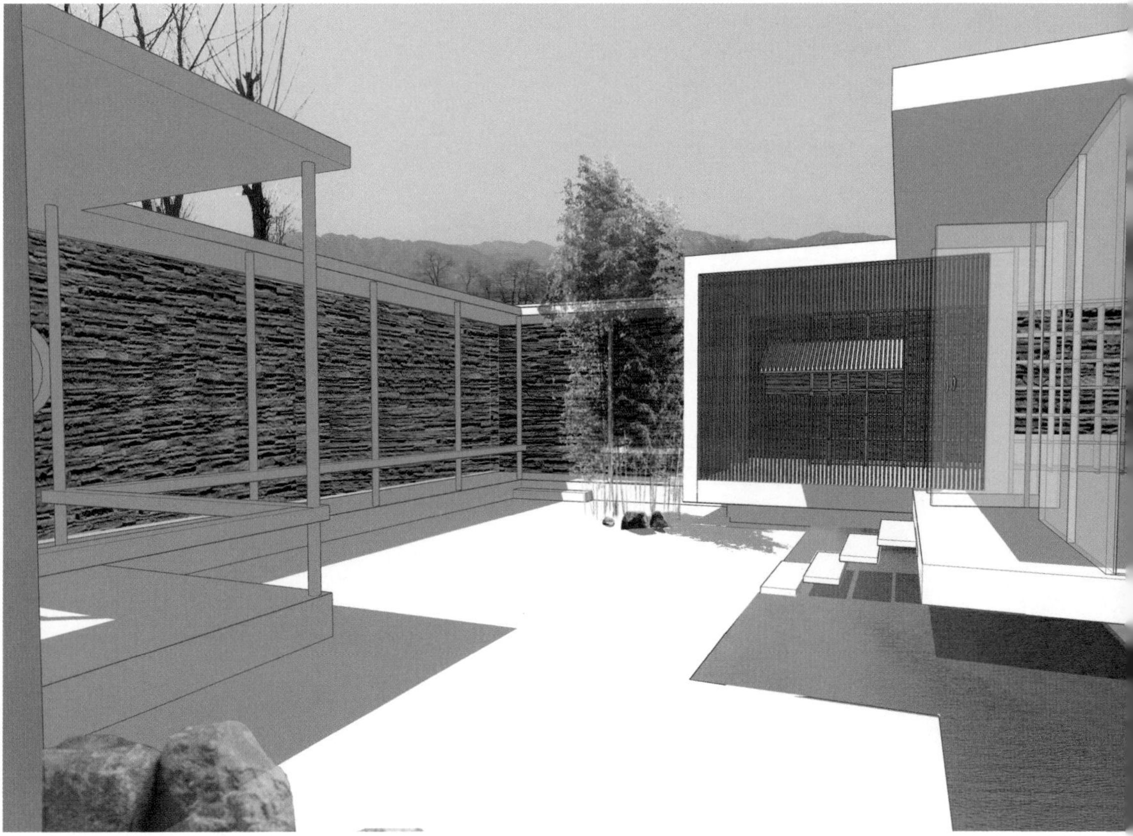

Project Chinese Villa Masterplan & Design, (competition) Beijing | **Location** South to Badaling Superhighway, Changping District, Beijing
Purpose residential | **Area** 100,000 m^2 (site: 30 ha) | **Design** 2005

UNITED DESIGN STUDIO

Cheng Yongyi
Wang Wenbin
Wang Gang
Sun Xiao
Xia Ruoxiang

www.uds.com.cn

This practice, with offices in Shanghai and Beijing, has specialised in town planning, public buildings and residential premises. It also provides consultation services, interior design and engineering services. The company's clear orientation towards the booming real estate market, above all in China's big cities, has resulted in a very varied portfolio that reveals many a reference to traditional Chinese construction styles but also a rich mix of international, predominantly western, forms and styles. The interaction of old and out-dated Chinese settlement structures with new forms of architecture representing old Europe is very popular in China's residential market, to such an extent that the echoes of old European, Mediterranean villa styles or English terraced housing districts have already found their enthusiastic adherents. More daring are the designs for public buildings, which are also adding a dash of the post-modern to China's new architecture.

Das Büro mit Sitz in Shanghai und Peking hat sich auf Städtebau, öffentliche Gebäude sowie Wohnbau spezialisiert und bietet außerdem Beratung sowie Innenarchitektur und Ingenieurdienstleistungen an. Die klare Ausrichtung am wachsenden Immobilienmarkt vor allem in chinesischen Großstädten hat ein sehr buntes Portfolio gezeitigt, in dem sich vielfältige Bezüge zu chinesischen Bautraditionen finden, aber gleichzeitig auch eine reichhaltige Mixtur internationaler, eher westlicher Formen und Stile. Die Konfrontation der alten, überholten chinesischen Siedlungsstrukturen mit neuen, traditionell europäischen Formen ist auf dem chinesischen Wohnungsmarkt sehr populär; so dass auch die formalen Bezüge zu mediterranem Villenstil oder englischen Reihenhaussiedlungen ihre Liebhaber gefunden haben. Formal gewagter sind die Entwürfe für öffentliche Bauten, die auch ein Stück Postmoderne nach China bringen.

▲
Project American Rock | **Location** No. 16, Baiziwan road, Chaoyang Distric, Beijing | **Purpose** residential | **Area** 565,081 m²
Design/Completion 10.2002/03.2005 | **Architect** Wang Gang

▶
Project Fuli City | **Location** Guangqumenwai Avenue, Beijing | **Purpose** residential | **Area** 1,353,000 m² | **Design** 10.2002
Architect Cheng Yongyi, Wang Wenbin, Wang Min, Liu Liming | **Associate** Baitao Hong Kong

◄ ▲
Project Sunco Sing & Sea
Location Huangcun, Daxing District, Beijing
Purpose residential
Area 518,586 m^2
Design 01.2004
Architect Cheng Yongyi, Xia Ruoxiang, Wang Wenbin, Zhang Xin, Wang Ting

»Mediterranean impressions« from Beijing
»Mediterrane Impressionen« aus Peking

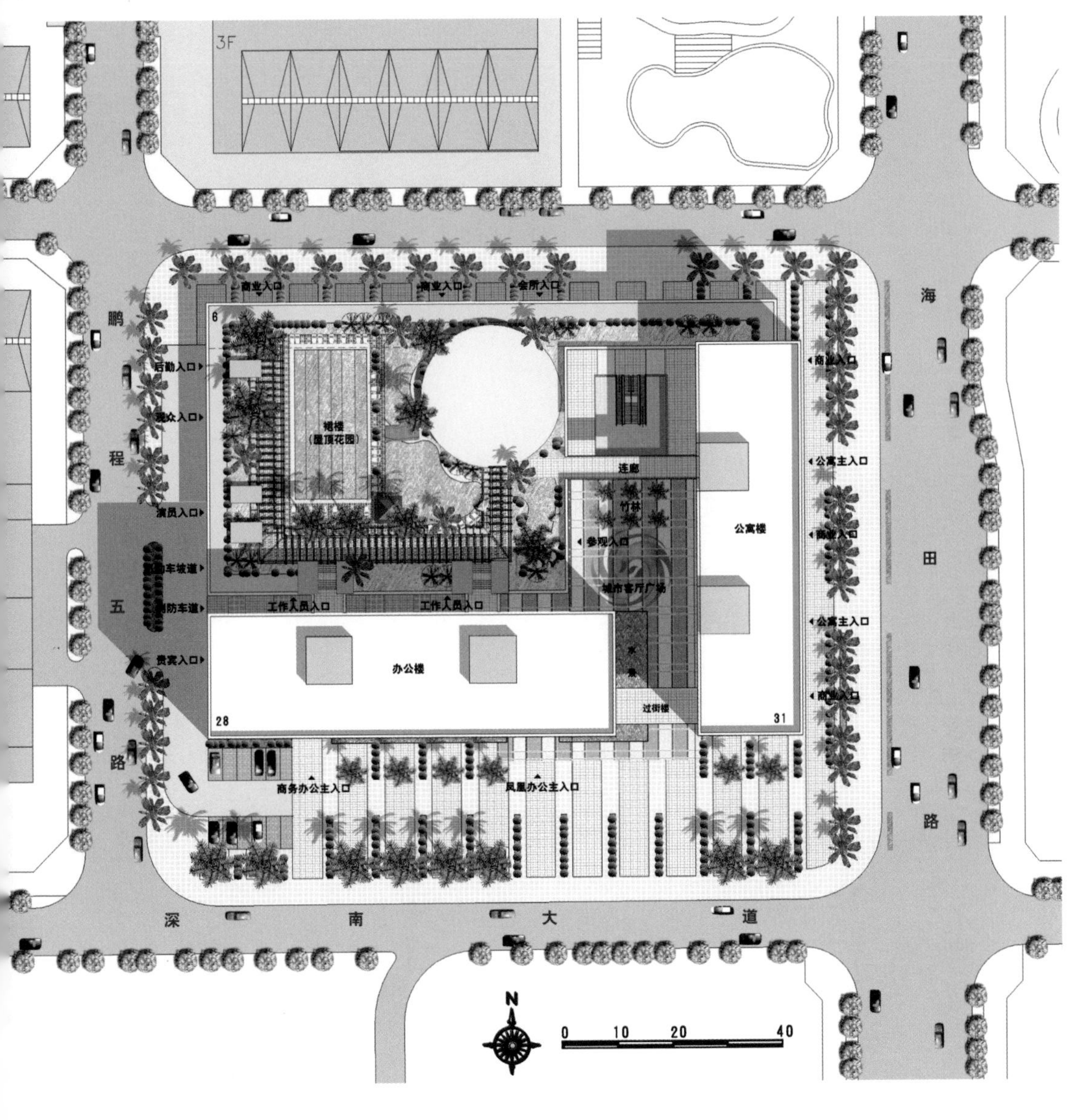

Project Tower of Phoenix TV headquarters
Location Shennan Avenue, Shenzhen
Purpose TV station, offices, residential
Area 110,950 m^2
Design 01.2004
Architect Cheng Yongyi, Wang Gang, Wang Wenbin

WERKHART INTERNATIONAL

Tao Tao
Lu Qiu
Yan Tao
Leng Jinsheng
Liu Li

www.werkhart.com

This multinational company with offices not only in Beijing, Shanghai, Hong Kong but also in Frankfurt, London and Melbourne is one of the largest, globally active architecture firms in the country, employing more than 200 people in China alone. The company focuses on sustainable planning and construction concepts and is one of the few architecture firms to acknowledge that the unbridled economic growth of the country is also destroying the natural environment and many old local and regional traditions. With this in mind the company's architects strive not only to build according to ecological guidelines but also to achieve some form of reconciliation between the huge nationwide drive to build and China's cultural heritage. The company also draws up concepts aiming at social and environmentally acceptable urbanisation processes that will lead to a fundamental change in the relationship between town and countryside.

Das multinationale Unternehmen mit Büros in Peking, Shanghai, Hongkong sowie in Frankfurt, London und Melbourne gehört zu den größten global agierenden Architekturbüros des Landes. Allein in China beschäftigt es mehr als 200 Mitarbeiter. Das Büro setzt auf nachhaltige Planungs- und Baukonzepte und ist eines der wenigen, die das ungebremste Wachstum der Wirtschaft des Landes für die anhaltende Zerstörung des natürlichen Lebensraums sowie alter lokaler und regionaler Traditionen verantwortlich machen. Vor diesem Hintergrund streben die Architekten nicht nur nach ökologischen Konzepten für Architektur und Städtebau, sondern versuchen auch, die massive Bautätigkeit im Land mit dem kulturellen Erbe zu versöhnen. Das Büro erarbeitet Konzepte für sozial- und umweltverträgliche Verstädterungsprozesse, die in China zu einer grundlegenden Veränderung des Verhältnisses von Stadt und Land führen.

▲▶

Project Jocund Garden Clubhouse, Beijing | **Location** Asian Games Village, Chaoyang District, Beijing
Purpose leisure | **Area** 2,500 m² | **Design/Completion** 09.2002/04.2004 | **Architect** Liu Li

Project Bluetooth Crystal – Shenzhen Futian Science and Technology Plaza
Location Shennan street, Shenzhen
Purpose offices
Area 256,000 m²
Design 01.2004
Architect Lu Qiu
Structural Design Werner Sobek Ingenieure GmbH
Ecological Design Transsolar Energietechnik GmbH

Project Zhongjiang Intercontinental Hotel
Location Changshu, Jiangsu Province
Purpose hotel
Area 42,786 m^2
Design/Completion 09.2003/2005
Architect Leng Jinsheng

Project Longgang Shopping Mall
Location Shenzhen Center
Purpose retail trade
Area 114,300 m²
Design 06.2003
Architect Lu Qiu

Project Sunville No. 1 House
Location Sheshan Mountain, National Tourism Park, Songjiang District, Shanghai
Purpose residential
Area 1,461 m^2
Design 02.2002
Architect Liu Li, Yan Tao

ATELIER 100S+1

▼

Peng Lele
Xu Yixing
Wang Xin
Huang Yi

▶ www.100s-1.com

The Beijing office was founded in 2001 and provides a platform for young architects sharing a common conception of traditional Chinese architecture. The company's young planners amass experience designing buildings and landscapes. In addition to the work itself a key feature of the office is its ongoing dialogue on methodologies and design approaches. Not only do the architects compile finely illustrated publications of their work; they also systematically collect samples of different materials, structures and surface finishes.

Das Pekinger Büro wurde im Jahr 2001 gegründet und bietet jungen Architekten Raum, die ein durchaus eigenes Verständnis traditioneller chinesischer Architektur eint. Ihre architektonische Praxis entwickeln die jungen Planer über das Entwerfen von Gebäuden und Landschaften. Neben der Arbeit selbst gehört der permanente Diskurs über Methoden und Entwurfsansätze zu den prägenden Eigenschaften des Büros. Die Architekten tragen nicht nur Bild- und Architekturbildbände zusammen, sondern sammeln systematisch auch Proben von Materialien, Strukturen und Oberflächen.

▲
Project OCEANPIC Digital Graphic Office, Beijing; renovation | **Location** Beijing | **Purpose** offices | **Area** 1,500 m²
Design/Completion 02–06.2004/06.2004 | **Project Manager** Peng Lele | **Architect** Xu Yixing, Wang Xin, He Chunyab, Xing Di

▶
Project Anqing Book City | **Location** Baiziqiao, South Jixiang road, Anqing, Anhui Province
Purpose library | **Area** 12,000 m² | **Design/Completion** 10.2003/10.2004 | **Project Manager** Peng Lele
Architect Xu Yixing, Wang Xin, Zhao Xiaoyu, Xing Di | **Associate** The 2nd. Architectural Institute, Anqing

◀▼▶

Project My Villa C-17
Location Southeast of the Yang Song Feng Xianghuan Island, Huai Rou, Beijing
Purpose residential
Area 238.9 m^2
Design/Completion 02.2005/08.2005
Project Manager Peng Lele
Architect Wang Xin, Wang Enli, Lin Chunguang, Li Zheng
Constructor Jianxue Architecture & Engineering Institute Co., Ltd.

▲◀
Chinese »Continental Style«
Chinesischer »Kontinentalstil«

SCENIC ARCHITECTURE

Zhu Xiaofeng

▸ office@scenicarch.com

Created in 2004 in Shanghai this practice has quickly made a name for itself with high-quality projects, particularly in the area of public buildings and town planning. Globalisation – which in the world of architecture means the import and export of form, materials and aesthetic concepts – poses a special challenge to the company. In the light of an increasing homogenisation of architecture, primarily in the larger, more spectacular projects involving cultural buildings or sports arenas, the architects see their role as designers of projects that incorporate local or regional culture and use the latter as a source of inspiration. They are convinced that buildings will then emerge that satisfy modern and international aspirations without denying their origins.

Das 2004 in Shanghai gegründete Büro hat sich mit seinen qualitätsvollen Projekten, vor allem im Bereich öffentlicher Bauten und Städtebau, rasch einen Namen gemacht. Die Globalisierung, im Falle der Architektur also eine Art Import und Export von Formen, Materialien und ästhetischen Konzepten, bedeutet für das Büro eine besondere Herausforderung. Angesichts einer zunehmenden Gleichschaltung der Architektur, hauptsächlich im Falle von größeren, spektakulären Projekten wie Kulturbauten oder Sportarenen, sehen die Architekten ihre Aufgabe darin, ihre Entwürfe mit einer bestimmten lokalen oder regionalen Kultur zu verknüpfen und Letztere als Quell der Inspiration zu betrachten. Auf diese Weise, so die Überzeugung, entsteht Architektur, die modernen und internationalen Ansprüchen genügt, jedoch ihre Herkunft nicht verleugnet.

▲ ▲ ▼

Project Renjie Riverfront Club | **Location** Qingpu, Shanghai | **Purpose** leisure | **Area** 1,070 m^2 | **Design** 12.2004

Project Qing Song Wai Garden
Location Qingpu, Shanghai
Purpose landscape architecture, restaurants
Area 1,603 m^2
Design/Completion 10.2004/07.2005
Architects Zhu Xiaofeng, Guo Dan

Two renovated buildings on 30,000 square metres green land, situated not far from the highway from Shanghai to Zhujiajiao.

Unweit des Highways von Shanghai nach Zhujiajio befinden sich auf etwa 30.000 Quadratmetern Grünfläche diese zwei Gebäude, bei deren Renovierung vor allem einheimische Materialien verwendet wurden.

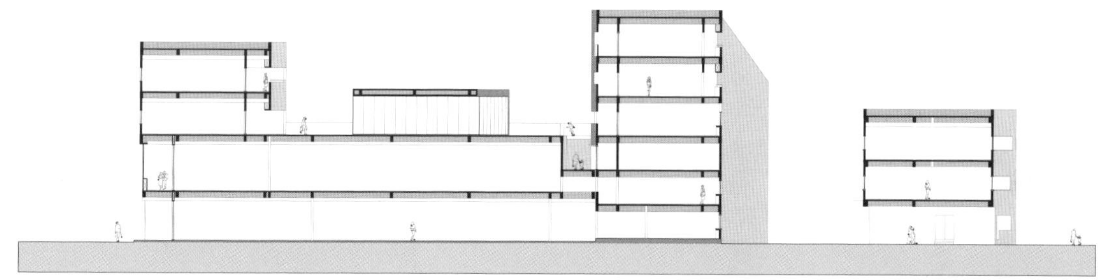

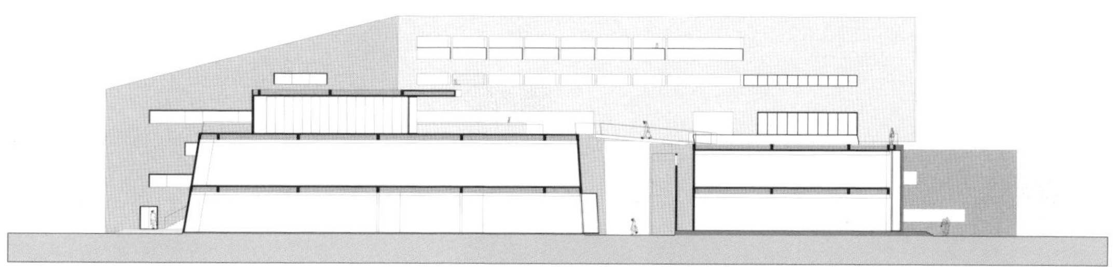

◀
Project Xiayang Lake Lot 6 (urban design)
Location Qingpu, Shanghai
Purpose hotel, offices, retail trade
Area 88,560 m²
Design 08.2004
Architects Zhu Xiaofeng, Guo Zhenxin, Lai Jiangsi, Yan Jun

▶
Project Chunshen Vanke Community Center
Location Shanghai
Purpose community services, post office, police station, restaurants, retail trade, offices etc.
Area 13,695 m²
Design/Completion 10.2004/2006

SHENZHEN X-URBAN ARCHITECTURAL DESIGN

Fei Xiaohua
Jia Dong
Deng Binzhu
Yu Tao
Shen Hua
Wang Bin
Ye Defeng

www.x-urban.com

This young architectural bureau is noted for a decidedly international approach, which profits from the qualified employees' wide variety of experience in the Western world, especially in the United States. The architects, urban planners and landscape designers, all graduates of the renowned Tongji University, are united in their ambition to not only offer architectural quality, but to have an influence on the various locations with their designs. Holistic thinking marks the different projects so far realised; these make no secret of their relatedness to the »white modernism« of the West. The founders strive to create an unmistakeably individual style with their architecture, which is intended to be noticed beyond the boundaries of China. Their buildings are meant to create just as much of an identity for the residents as they do for the architects responsible for them.

Das junge Büro zeichnet sich durch einen betont internationalen Ansatz aus, der von den vielfältigen Erfahrungen der qualifizierten Mitarbeiter im westlichen Ausland, insbesondere den Vereinigten Staaten, profitiert. Die Architekten, Stadtplaner und Landschaftsgestalter; allesamt Absolventen der renommierten Tongji-Universität, verbindet der Ehrgeiz, nicht nur architektonische Qualität anzubieten, sondern mit den Entwürfen auch Einfluss auf die Entwicklung der jeweiligen Orte zu nehmen. Ganzheitliches Denken prägt die verschiedenartigen, bislang realisierten Projekte, die ihre Wahlverwandtschaft mit der »Weißen Moderne« des Westens nicht verhehlen. Mit ihrer Architektur streben die Gründer des Büros nicht zuletzt nach einer unverwechselbaren Handschrift, die auch über die Grenzen von China hinaus wahrgenommen werden soll. Ihre Bauten sollen für die Bewohner ebenso identifikationsstiftend sein wie für die Architekten, die dafür verantwortlich sind.

▲▶

Project Public toilet at the top of Lianhua Mountain Park | **Location** Lianhua Mountain Park, Shenzhen
Purpose public bathroom | **Design** 05.2002 | **Architect** Fei Xiaohua, Shen Hua, Pan Houli

0 1 3 5

▲▶
Project Shiyan Art & Sport Center | **Location** Shenzhen
Purpose culture, leisure | **Area** 12,000 m^2 | **Design** 07.2003
Architect Fei Xiaohua, Deng Bingzhu, Zhuang Minghui

▼
Project Nanshan Mountain Art Museum | **Location** Shenzhen
Purpose museum | **Area** 36,000 m^2 | **Design** 09.2004
Architect Fei Xiaohua, Jia Dong, Deng Bingzhu, Zhu Dongyan

4F
育
才
路
龙
腾
环
总平面图
0 5 20m

▲
Project A proposal of urban design for Yiwu
Location Yiwu, Zhejiang Province
Purpose culture, leisure
Area 9,000 m²
Design 06.2002–09.2002
Architect Jia Dong, Ye Defeng

◄
Project Guangdong Seaside Vacation Villa
Location Guangdong Province
Purpose residential
Area 500 m²
Design/Completion 2003/10.2003
Architect Fei Xiaohua, Li Xinhua, Xia Yuan, Huang An

INCREDIBLES

UNITED DESIGN GROUP

Bo Xi

Wang Maoting

Lin Zhenhong

Chuan Wang

▶ **www.udg.com.cn**

This office is one of the leading architecture firms in China and can point to a list of successful projects in practically every area of the profession. The company provides not only architectural and urban planning services but also engineering expertise, interior design, consultation services and project development. Its commercial success can be attributed in part to the high architectural standards of the designs, which reflect the artistic bent of their creators. These unquantifiable attributes have won the firm numerous awards and prizes. One of the secrets of this very measurable success consists in the innovative work processes that the company has adopted. A growing number of employees has led to the formation of small design teams focussed on a single task and working within an atmosphere of creativity.

Das Büro zählt zu den führenden Architekturfirmen Chinas und kann auf erfolgreiche Projekte in nahezu allen Bereichen verweisen. Neben Architektur und Stadtplanung zählen Ingenieurleistungen, Innenarchitektur sowie Beratung und Projektentwicklung zum Angebotsspektrum des Unternehmens. Der kommerzielle Erfolg hat auch mit dem hohen architektonischen Niveau der Entwürfe zu tun, die den künstlerischen Anspruch ihrer Schöpfer widerspiegeln. Diese nicht messbaren Qualitäten zeitigten zahlreiche Wettbewerbspreise und Prämierungen. Ein Geheimnis dieses wiederum messbaren Erfolgs besteht in der innovativen Arbeitsweise des Büros. Angesichts der wachsenden Mitarbeiterzahl wurden kleine Entwurfsteams gebildet, die sich in einer kreativen Atmosphäre konzentriert einer bestimmten Aufgabe widmen können.

▲
Project Nanjing Hexi Commercial Center | **Location** Nanjing
Purpose retail trade, offices, hotel | **Area** 500,000m² | **Design/Completion** 2006/2010 | **Architect** Wang Chuan, Diao Rui

▶
Project Wuxi Media Tower | **Location** Wuxi | **Purpose** offices, hotels, retail trade
Area 200,000 m² | **Design/Completion** 12.2006/12.2008 | **Architect** Bo Xi, Yan Zongjie, in collaboration with gmp

▶
Project Wuxi Jiade Central Park Residential
Location Wuxi
Purpose residential
Area 150,000 m^2
Design/Completion 2004/2005
Architect Bo Xi, Zhou Haibiao

▼
Project Tianjin Friendship Xintiandi
Location Tianjin
Purpose retail trade
Area 100,000 m^2
Design/Completion 2004/2005
Architect Wang Chuan, Wang Yu, Chen Fei

▶
Project Wuxi Museum
Location Wuxi
Purpose museum
Area: 450,000 m^2
Design 10.2005
Architect Wang Chuan, Huang Fan, in collaboration with PES

▲
Project Wuxi Lihu Government Center
Location Wuxi
Purpose offices, retail trade | **Area** 100,000 m^2
Design 2004
Architect Bo Xi, Wang Chuan, Zhou Xiaobo

▲
Project Shanghai Vanke Blue Mountain
Location Shanghai
Purpose residential | **Area** 675,000 m^2
Design/Completion 10.2005/10.2007
Architect Wang Chuan, Song Haiqing, in collaboration with PES

Project Shanghai Electronic Town
Location Shanghai
Purpose offices, retail trade | **Area** 260,000 m^2
Design/Completion 05.2004/12.2006
Architect Bo Xi, Wang Maoting, Gu Zhipeng, Zhou Xiaobo

STANDARDARCHITECTURE

▼

Zhang Ke
Zhang Hong
Ru Lei
Claudia Taborda

▶ www.standardarchitecture.cn

This office, set up in 1999, employs young designers and architects with international experience in the areas of landscape architecture, building design, interior design and product/industrial design. Following a steep rise in the number of competitions won in China the studio upped stakes from New York in 2001 and moved to Beijing, setting up shop in a historic renovated warehouse adjacent to the University. The office's projects combine traditional Chinese elements with the international modern style.

In dem 1999 gegründeten Büro arbeiten junge, international erfahrene Designer und Architekten aus den Bereichen Landschaftsarchitektur, Architektur, Innenarchitektur sowie Produkt- und Industriedesign zu-sammen. Nachdem das ursprünglich in New York ansässige Studio mehr und mehr Wettbewerbe in China gewonnen hatte, zog es im Jahr 2001 nach Peking um, wo es heute in einem renovierten historischen Lagerhaus in unmittelbarer Nähe zur Universität sitzt. In seinen Projekten verbindet es traditionelle chinesische Elemente mit der internationalen Moderne.

Project SA Workshop
Location Academy of Science Factory Compound, Beijing
Purpose offices
Area 340 m² (**Site Area** 500 m²)
Design/Completion 2004
Architect Zhang Hong, Zhang Ke

A renovated historic factory building is the new studio of standardarchitecture.
Das neue Büro von standardarchitecture: ein behutsam renoviertes historisches Lagerhaus.

Project Storefronts in Yangshuo
Location Yangshuo, Guilin
Purpose retail trade
Area 6,254 m²
(**Site Area** 2 366 m²)
Design/Completion 2003–2004/
05.2004–05.2005
Architect Zhang Hong, Zhang Ke,
Claudia Taborda
Team Gai Xudong, Du Xiaomin,
Yang Ying, Qi Honghai,
Han Xiaowei, Hao Zengrui,
Qing Ying, Liang Hua,
Wang Wenxiang, Liu Xinjie

Yangshuo Storefronts: local materials and construction methods.
Yangshuo Storefronts: einheimische Baumaterialien und Konstruktionsmethoden.

OTHERS-STUDIO

Yang Yin
Gao Dezhan
Zhang Yining

▶ www.others.cn

Other by name, other by nature. The three young architects – one woman, two men – are not simply on a quest for »otherness« in architecture; they are also acutely attuned to the wishes and expectations of the other party, the client, be it the commissioning owner or the eventual user. The office was founded in 1998 and has made a name for itself above all through its important construction projects in the residential and commercial sectors and its planning work on behalf of public clients.

Der Name des Büros ist Programm. Die drei jungen Architekten – eine Frau und zwei Männer – sind nicht nur auf der Suche nach dem anderen, alternativen Ausdruck in der Architektur, sondern haben auch immer die Wünsche und Erwartungen des Anderen, des Gegenübers im Blick; egal ob Bauherr oder Nutzer. Das Büro wurde 1998 gegründet und ist vor allem durch seine größeren Projekte im Bereich Wohnungs- und Geschäftsbau sowie durch Planungen für öffentliche Auftraggeber bekannt geworden.

▲▶

Project College of Theatre's Art, Shenyang Normal University | **Location** Shenyang, Liaoning Province | **Purpose** education
Area 21,974 m^2 | **Design/Completion** 02.2004/08.2005 | **Architect** Yang Yin, Zhang Yining, Gao Dezhan, Sun Qiang

▼▶
Project Yantong Temple
Location Mingshan Island, Luobei County, Heilongjiang Province
Purpose religion
Area 48,000 m^2
Design/Completion 05.2003
Architect Yang Yin, Gao De Zhan, Zhang Yining

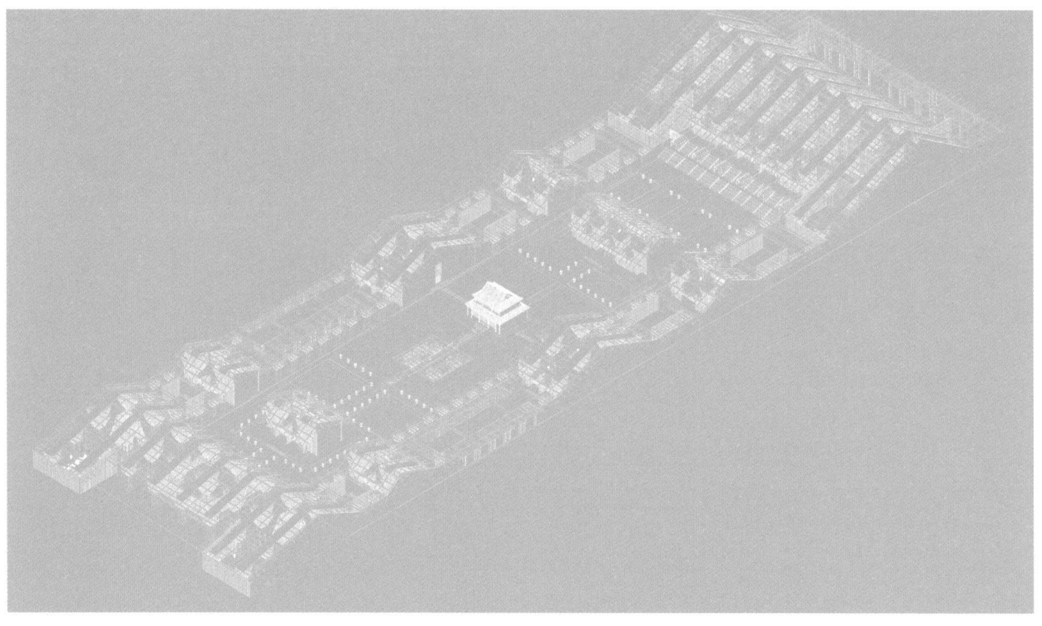

山门殿后外庭

Project Fashion Research Development and Manufacture Base
Location Shenyang, Liaoning Province
Purpose offices
Area 13,796 m^2
Design/Completion 05.2004/08.2005
Architect Yang Yin, Zhang Yining, Sun Qiang

MO CHEN ARCHITECTS AND ENGINEERS

Wang Hui

Lai Jun

▶ www.mochen.com.cn

The name of the practice could be rendered in English as »pious designers«, an appropriate label for a group of architects who feel bound by certain ideals and beliefs. Founded in 1995, the company was one of the first private architecture practices, in 2002, to be granted official status in Beijing. The tension – typical for the new China – between the immensely popular western architecture and traditional building forms provides the setting for the firm's quest for a way to rehabilitate form, colour and materials, all of which are threatened by a creeping homogenisation of modern Chinese architecture. In the eyes of the firm's owners architectural diversity is in as much danger as the biodiversity found in nature. They have made it their task to preserve the richness and viability of this diversity of building styles.

Der Name des Büros bedeutet soviel wie »fromme Designer« und ist insofern recht zutreffend, als hier Architekten arbeiten, die sich bestimmten Idealen und Überzeugungen verpflichtet fühlen. Gegründet 1995, gehörte das Büro im Jahr 2002 zu den ersten anerkannten privaten Unternehmen in dieser Branche in Peking. In einem für das neue China typischen Spannungsverhältnis zwischen der ungemein populären westlichen Architektur und alten Bautraditionen sucht das Büro nach einem Weg, Formen, Materialien und Farben zu rehabilitieren, die im Zuge einer Art von Gleichschaltung der modernen chinesischen Architektur zu verschwinden drohen. Für die Inhaber des Büros ist die Vielfalt der Baukunst auf ähnliche Weise bedroht wie der Artenreichtum der belebten Natur. Diesen Schatz zu bewahren und lebensfähig zu erhalten, ist das Ziel ihrer Arbeit.

▲▶▼

Project Shijia Primary School
Location Dongcheng District, Beijing | **Purpose** education | **Area** 31,000 m² | **Design/Completion** 2002/2002

▲◀▼
Views of the new campus
Der neue Campus, Ansichten

▶ ▼
Project Wanke Green Garden
Location Chaoyang District, Beijing
Purpose residential
Area 300,000 m²
Design/Completion 12.2002/2003

Project Wanke West Hill Garden
Location Xiaojiahe, Haidian District, Beijing
Purpose residential | **Area** 144,000 m²
Design/Completion 2003/2004

Various views of the green courtyard
Der grüne Innenhof, verschiedene Ansichten

SILVER COURT
5383 7128
SILVER TOWER
5383 6555

COAST PALISADE CONSULTING GROUP

Qiu Jiang

Mei Mei

Matthew Mander

▶ www.cpcgroupsh.com

This company was created in 1994 in Vancouver, Canada, and has been active in the Chinese market since 1995. With upwards of 50 employees working at home and abroad Coast Palisade offers both public and private clients an array of services encompassing architecture, town planning, landscape planning and interior design. In 2001 the company opened a branch in Shanghai. The architects' work is informed not only by a respect for China and its ancient traditions but also by a detailed grasp of the radical changes currently occurring in the country. CPC designs, in their interpretive dimension, have featured among the success stories of western architecture in China.

Das Büro wurde 1994 in Vancouver, Kanada gegründet und ist seit 1995 auf dem chinesischen Markt tätig. Mit seinen mehr als 50 in- und ausländischen Mitarbeitern offeriert es staatlichen wie auch privatwirtschaftlich organisierten Auftraggebern ein umfassendes Leistungsangebot in den Bereichen Architektur, Stadt- und Landschaftsplanung sowie Innenarchitektur. Im Jahr 2001 wurde eine Filiale des Büros in Shanghai eröffnet. Die Arbeit der Architekten ist nicht allein von Respekt vor China und seinen alten Traditionen geprägt, sondern auch von Verständnis für die gegenwärtige Umbruchsituation. Der große Erfolg westlicher Architektur geht auch in die Entwürfe von CPC ein; gleichwohl in einer interpretativen Art und Weise.

▲▶
Project Silver Tower
Location Huaihai road, Shanghai
Purpose offices
Area 60,000 m^2
Design/Completion 2001/2004
Architect Qui Jiang, Mei Mei, Matthew Mander

 Interior view

 Innenansicht

▲◄
Project Chongqing Complex
Location Chongqing
Purpose retail trade, hotel, offices
Area 700,000 m²
Design/Completion 2003/2007
Architect Chen Wenxiong, Matthew Mander

Project ZhengDa Cube Edifice
Location Shanghai
Purpose offices
Area 41,000 m²
Design/Completion 2004/2007
Architect Qiu Jiang, Chen Wenxiong

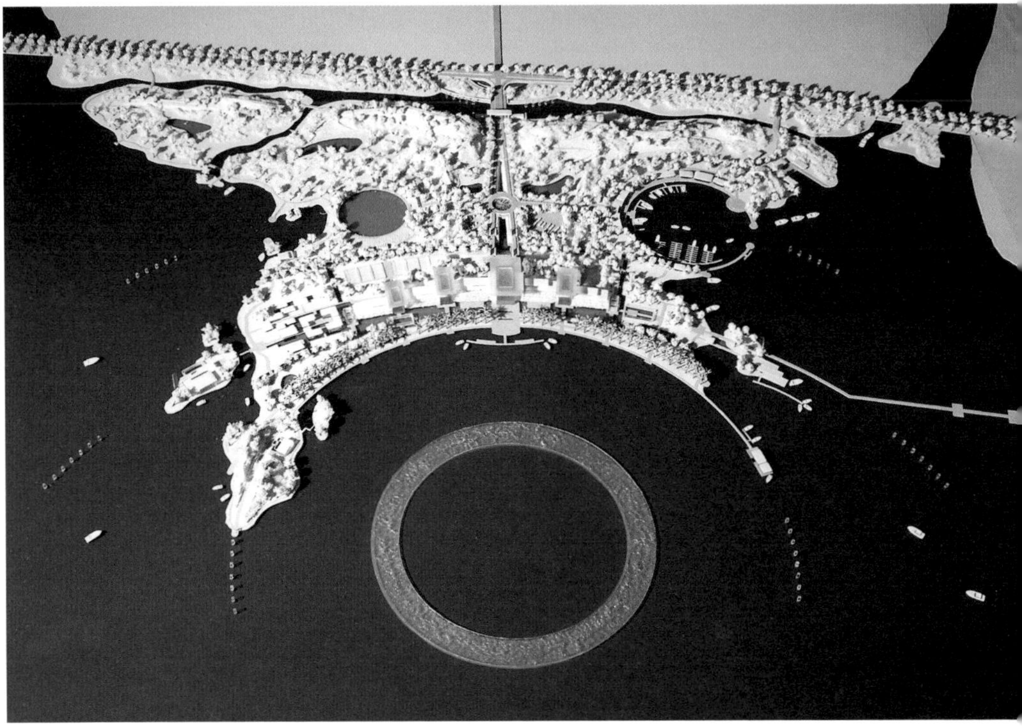

▲
Project Jinji Lake Hotel (Ultra 5 Star)
Location Suzhou
Purpose hotel
Area 103,231 m^2
Design 2003
Architect Qiu Jiang
Cooperator Arthur Erichson

Project Dalian Cultural Center
Location Dalian Economic and Technical Development Zone, Liaoning
Purpose culture, entertainment
Area 80,000 m²
Design/Completion 2002/2006
Architect Qiu Jiang, Matthew Mander, Arthur Erichson

ZHEJIANG SOUTH ARCHITECTURAL DESIGN

▼

Fang Zhida

▶ south@mail.hz.zj.cn

This architecture firm, founded in 1999, has developed a multifaceted corporate structure and now employs upwards of 138 people in a total of four locations. It boasts four design departments, two planning departments, a logistics office, a landscape planning office, 2D and 3D departments and a technical service centre. The services it provides are fully geared to the Chinese market and have expanded to reflect developments in the country's real estate market. Despite the march of western architecture the company's planners set great store on respecting China's regional construction traditions and take pains to combine conventional local styles with innovative architecture.

Das 1999 gegründete Büro hat eine differenzierte Unternehmensstruktur aufgebaut und beschäftigt über 138 Mitarbeiter an insgesamt vier Standorten. Es verfügt über vier Entwurfsabteilungen, zwei Abteilungen für Bauplanung, ein Büro für Versorgungsplanung, ein Landschaftsplanungsbüro, 2-D- und 3-D-Abteilungen sowie ein Zentrum für technischen Service. Die Leistungen und Angebote sind strikt auf den chinesischen Markt ausgerichtet und wurden mit dem sich entwickelnden Immobilienmarkt des Landes immer differenzierter. Trotz des anhaltenden Siegeszuges einer westlich geprägten Architektur respektieren die Planer des Büros die chinesischen regionalen Bautraditionen und streben nach einer Verbindung von lokaltypischen Formen und innovativer Architektur.

▲▶

Project Suzhou Courts | **Location** Old Town, Suzhou
Purpose residential | **Area** 100,000 m^2 | **Design/Completion** 02.2003/09.2005 | **Architect** Fang Zhida, Lin Song, Yu Yongbin

◄▲

Project A Street of Interest by the Lake
Location Lakeside District, Hangzhou, Zhenjiang Province
Purpose offices, retail trade, residential, leisure
Area 50,000 m²
Design/Completion 10.2002–03.2003/10.2003
Architect Fang Zhida, Tian Yu, Sun Hang, Lou Haifeng

◄
Project Brand New World
Location Hunnan New Area, Shenyang, Liaoning Province
Purpose residential
Area 180,000 m^2
Design/Completion 05.2003/12.2005
Architect Fang Zhida, Ye Jianwei,
Deng Xiaojun, Wang Yuan

▼
Project BeiAnQinSen Residential Quarter
Location Ningbo, Zhejiang
Purpose residential
Area 300,000 m^2
Design/Completion 05.2003–03.2005/03.2006
Architect Fang Zhida, Lin Yong,
Wang Deng Yue, Wang Zhi

ARCHITECTURAL DESIGN & RESEARCH INSTITUTE

▼

Chen Hui
Mao Hongnian
Wang Dapeng
Dong Qing
Cui Guangya
Hong Haibo
Fang Li
Xie Geng
Zhu Zhenmin
Ge Lingyan
Shen Qiang
Tang Xuedong
Lai Hongyu
Fang Yunqing

Created in the early 1990s this firm now employs a staff of 530, most being qualified engineers and architects. Always geared to the needs of the market the office was quick to prosper. Its internal work processes have changed to reflect the sharp growth in contracts and employee numbers: the design and planning process is organised to fit the industry's more flexible working patterns, which now require continuous liaison between the various parties involved. This private planning office is keen to use its numerous international contacts, particularly in Canada and Japan, to tap into the global architecture market and, in doing so, assist in the opening up of China.

Das Büro, gegründet Anfang der Neunzigerjahre, hat inzwischen 530 Mitarbeiter; die meisten davon sind staatlich geprüfte Ingenieure und Architekten. Eine konsequente Ausrichtung nach den Erfordernissen des Marktes bescherte dem Unternehmen rasche Erfolge. Die interne Arbeitsweise hat sich durch den rasanten Zuwachs an Aufträgen wie auch an Angestellten inzwischen verändert: Die Abläufe des Entwurfs- und Planungsprozesses orientieren sich an den flexibilisierten Arbeitsrhythmen der Industrie, die einen ständigen Austausch zwischen den Beteiligten erfordern. Durch zahlreiche internationale Kontakte vor allem nach Kanada und Japan sucht das private Planungsunternehmen Anschluss an das globale Architekturgeschehen und möchte auf diese Weise auch die Öffnung Chinas befördern.

Project Xiasha New Campus, Hangzhou Teachers College | **Location** Xiasha, Hangzhou | **Purpose** education | **Area** 260,000 m²
Design/Completion 2001/2005 | **Architect** Zhu Zhenmin, Fang Yuanqing

Project Beilun Administration Center
Location Ningbo, Zhejiang
Purpose offices
Area 120,000 m²
Design/Completion 2002/2005
Architect Zhu Zhenmin, Wei Hongfeng, Fang Yuanqing

Project Zhongda Wu Village Stream of Space
Location Hangzhou
Purpose residential
Area 45,000 m²
Design/Completion 2000/2003
Architect Hong Haibo, Zhu Yongkang

European style condominium
Wohnanlage im europäischen Stil

S+Y ARCHITECTURE DESIGN

Sun Tongyu

Yu Yong

▶ www.stystudio.com

With its roots in a design professorship at Tongji University it is small wonder that this company values the link between theory and practice above all else. The design process is based on meticulous studies of architectural forms and is backed up by a detailed assessment of the location. The company's owners regard an analysis of the respective town, the architectural setting, the social environment and cultural and economic processes as a crucial aspect of a planning process that takes full account of the location's specific requirements. At the end of this process the concrete design – the building's form – emerges. The building's form is more than simply a style; it is at the core of what architecture is all about.

Hervorgegangen aus einem Lehrstuhl für Entwurf an der Tongji Universität, ist es kein Wunder, dass das Büro vor allem auf die Verbindung von Theorie und Praxis der Architektur Wert legt. Der Entwurfsprozess basiert auf exakten und gründlichen Studien von architektonischen Formen, denen sich die Untersuchung des konkreten Ortes anschließt. Eine Analyse der jeweiligen Stadt, des baulichen Kontextes, der sozialen Zusammenhänge und kulturellen wie ökonomischen Prozesse betrachten die Inhaber des Büros als unverzichtbaren Schritt hin zu einer Planung, die den spezifischen Anforderungen sowohl der gebauten als auch der belebten Umwelt gerecht wird. Aus all diesen Schritten ergibt sich dann der konkrete Entwurf, die Form. Sie ist mehr als nur Stil, sondern die Essenz dessen, was Architektur zu fassen hat.

▲▶
Project Six Villas of Zidujing Garden, Sheshan Mountain
Location Sichen Highway, Songjiang District, Shanghai
Purpose residential
Area 350–500 m² each | **Design** 2003

»Architectural design is designing life.« (S+Y Architecture Design)
»Architektur bedeutet das Leben zu gestalten.« (S+Y Architecture Design)

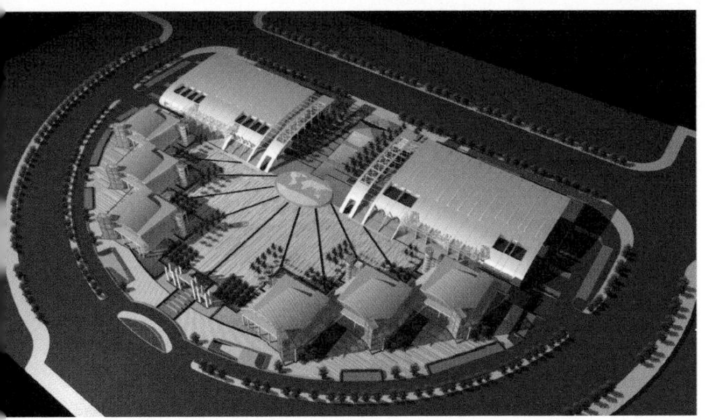

Project Wuyi Square Exhibition Center, Jiangmen
Location Wuyi street and Shishan road, Jiangmen, Guangdong Province
Purpose offices, exhibition spaces
Area 49,158 m^2
Design/Completion 2003/2005

Project Commercial and pedestrian street of Nice Land and Neighbour Garden
Location Gutang road, Pudong, Shanghai (near Jinhai road)
Purpose retail trade
Area 10,000 m²
Design/Completion 2003/2005

The aim of this project was to bring back the lost city life.

Ziel dieses Projekts war, eine reine Wohngegend mit Geschäften zu wiederzubeleben.

DAHUA
大华集团

SHANGHAI BROCH ARCHITECT ASSOCIATES

Liu Gang

Wan Jiangjiao

Qin Huahao

▶ bochuang@vip.sina.com

The office pools the talents of experienced, state-recognised architects all with considerable experience in the areas of publicly funded construction projects and residential property. The three architects behind the enterprise have all managed construction projects at home and abroad and have worked at a number of architecture institutes. The office's planners are at pains to develop their own recognisable signature and all regard the combination of international standards, technical innovation and local traditions on the ground as an opportunity for Chinese architecture to join the global debate.

Das Büro ist ein Zusammenschluss von staatlich anerkannten, erfahrenen Architekten, die auf reichhaltige Erfahrungen im Bereich öffentliches Bauen sowie Wohnungsbau zurückgreifen können.
Die drei führenden Köpfe des Büros haben Bauprojekte im In- und Ausland betreut und waren an verschiedenen Architekturinstituten tätig. In ihrer Arbeit streben die Planer nach einer wiedererkennbaren, eigenen Handschrift und sehen in der Verbindung von internationalen Standards, technischer Innovation und spezifischen lokalen Traditionen eine Möglichkeit, der chinesischen Architektur Anschluss an die globale Debatte zu verschaffen.

▲▶
Project Bin Jiang Ya Yuan
Location Hualing road, Shanghai
Purpose residential
Area 180,000 m^2
Design/Completion 03.2001/08.2004
Architect Liu Gang, Qin Huahao, Wan Jiangjia

Urban life along the river
Städtisches Leben am Fluss

DAHUA
大华集团

Project Seasons Town in Kunshan
Location Chinese Garden road, Kunshan
Purpose residential, landscape architecture
Area 250,000 m²
Design/Completion 05.2002/10.2005
Architect Liu Gang, Yang Bo, Yan Jin

Residential buildings with façades in vivid green and yellow shades.

Die Wohngebäude zeichnen sich durch eine lebendige Fassadengestaltung in frischen Grün- und Gelbtönen aus.

Project School of media and design in Shanghai Jiaotong University
Location Shanghai
Purpose education
Area 150,000 m²
Design/Completion 06.2003/11.2005
Architect Wan Jiangjiao, Yan Jin

Modern style for China's future designers.
Strenges, klares Design für die zukünftigen Gestalter Chinas.

DBLANT DESIGN INTERNATIONAL

Eric Zheng

Fanye Wang

Jessie Yan

▶ www.dblant.com

Created in 1995 with head offices in the USA the firm sees itself as a bridge between China and the West. The architects, many of whom are products of Europe or America, consider themselves as purveyors of modern architectural practices to China and also as promoters of a dialogue on the theory of modern architecture. The Shanghai office began modestly but now employs more than 50 people. Many of its projects have been covered in journals and books. In their designs the architects attempt to marry the wishes of the building owners and clients with their own ideals. The office is renowned above all for the plans it has produced for public buildings such as schools, universities, sports grounds and community centres.

Das Büro, gegründet 1995 und mit seinem Hauptsitz in den USA registriert, versteht sich als Brücke zwischen China und der westlichen Welt. Die Architekten, zum großen Teil mit einem in Europa und den USA geprägten Hintergrund, sehen ihre Aufgabe in China vor allem in der Vermittlung von moderner Architekturpraxis, aber auch in dem theoretischen Diskurs über moderne Baukunst. Während im Shanghaier Büro anfangs nur eine Handvoll Mitarbeiter beschäftigt waren, sind es heute weit über 50. Zahlreiche Projekte des Büros wurden in Zeitschriften und Büchern vorgestellt. In ihren Entwürfen versuchen die Architekten, die Wünsche der Bauherren und Auftraggeber mit ihren eigenen Idealen zu verknüpfen. Das Büro wurde vor allem für seine Planungen für öffentliche Gebäude wie Schulen, Universitäten, Sportstätten oder Gemeindezentren bekannt.

▲▲

▲

Project Yinzhou Science Center
Location Central Yinzhou District
Purpose offices, labs
Area 26,500 m²
Design/Completion 08.2002/07.2005
Architect Zheng Ke, Yan Jiahui, Ma Yingchun

▲▼

Project Ningbo Higher Education Park Gymnasium and Training Building
Location South Qianhu road, Yinzhou District, Ningbo
Purpose leisure, sports
Area 36,600 m²
Design/Completion 08.2001/08.2003
Architect Zheng Ke, Wang Fanye
Associate Zhejiang Architectural Design & Research Institute

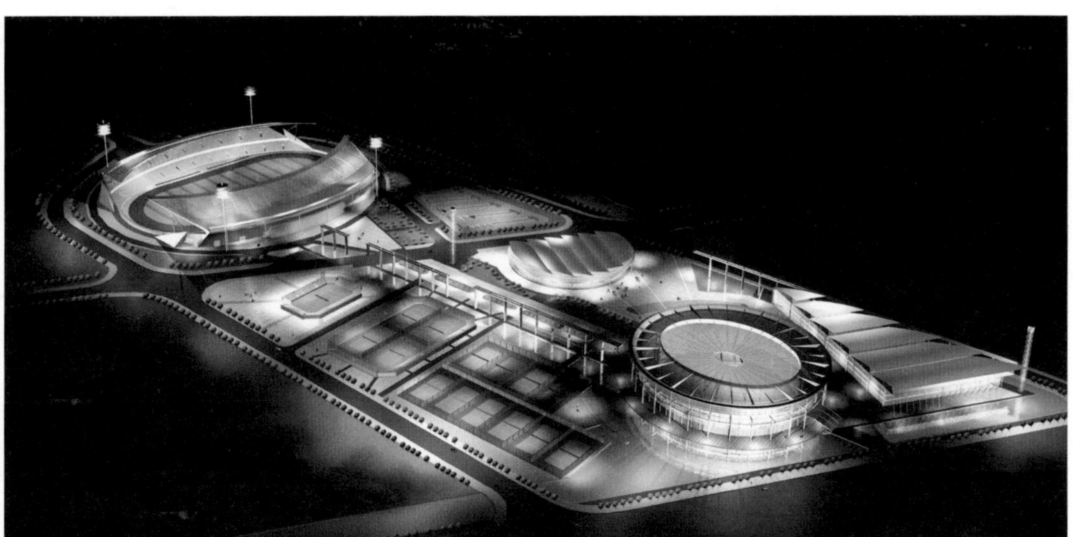

大学生中心透视图

Project Tianjin Institute of Urban Construction
Location Southwest Tianjin, outside the outer ring
Purpose education
Area 290,000 m^2
Design 01.2004
Architect Zheng Ke, Weng Bo

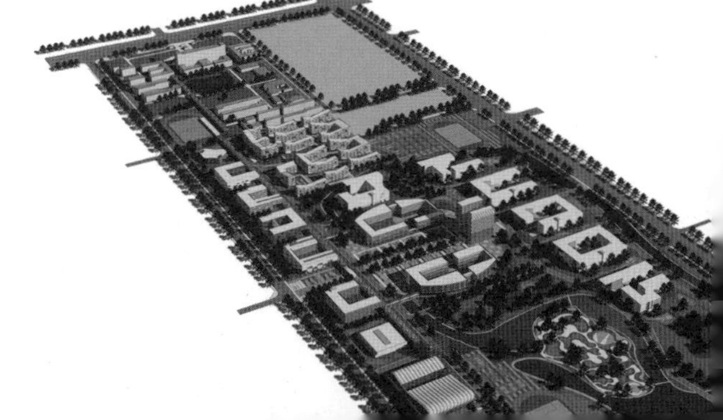

KingsMall
STRENGTH

CHEN SHI MIN ARCHITECTS

▼

Chen Shi Min

▶ www.chenshimin-arch.com

The architecture office was created in 1996 and maintains branches in mainland China and Hong Kong. Company founder Chen Shi Min is considered the grand old man of Chinese architecture and has amassed a 50 years of experience in the profession. Chen Shi Min's projects respect Chinese traditions while working to international standards. Besides carrying out the normal activities expected of an architecture firm Chen Shi Min also organises and monitors all aspects of the construction process itself and performs associated services. The practice boasts a reliable network of skilled partners and can also be consulted on post-construction after-sales issues and also on matters relating to renting and selling.

Das Büro, gegründet im Jahr 1996, hält Zweigstellen in China selbst sowie in Hongkong. Sein Gründer Chen Shi Min gilt als Nestor der chinesischen Architektur und kann mittlerweile auf mehr als 50 Jahre Berufserfahrung zurückblicken. Die Projekte von Chen Shi Min vereinen internationale Standards und chinesische Traditionen. Das Angebot des Büros umfasst allerdings nicht nur die üblichen Architektenleistungen, sondern schließt auch die gesamte Organisation und Überwachung des Bauprozesses sowie alle damit zusammenhängenden Dienstleistungen ein. Über ein zuverlässiges Netz aus kompetenten Partnern verfügend, steht das Büro nach Abschluss der Bauarbeiten auch für Fragen zum After-Sales-Service sowie zu Vermietung und Verkauf zur Verfügung.

▲▶
Project DiJing Mall
Location Chongqing
Purpose retail trade
Area 214,840 m^2
Design/Completion 2004

The 3rd-generation shopping center featuring »ecology, recreation and humanity«.
Entwurf für eine Shopping Mall der »dritten Generation«, das Ökologie, Freizeit und Soziales miteinander verbinden soll.

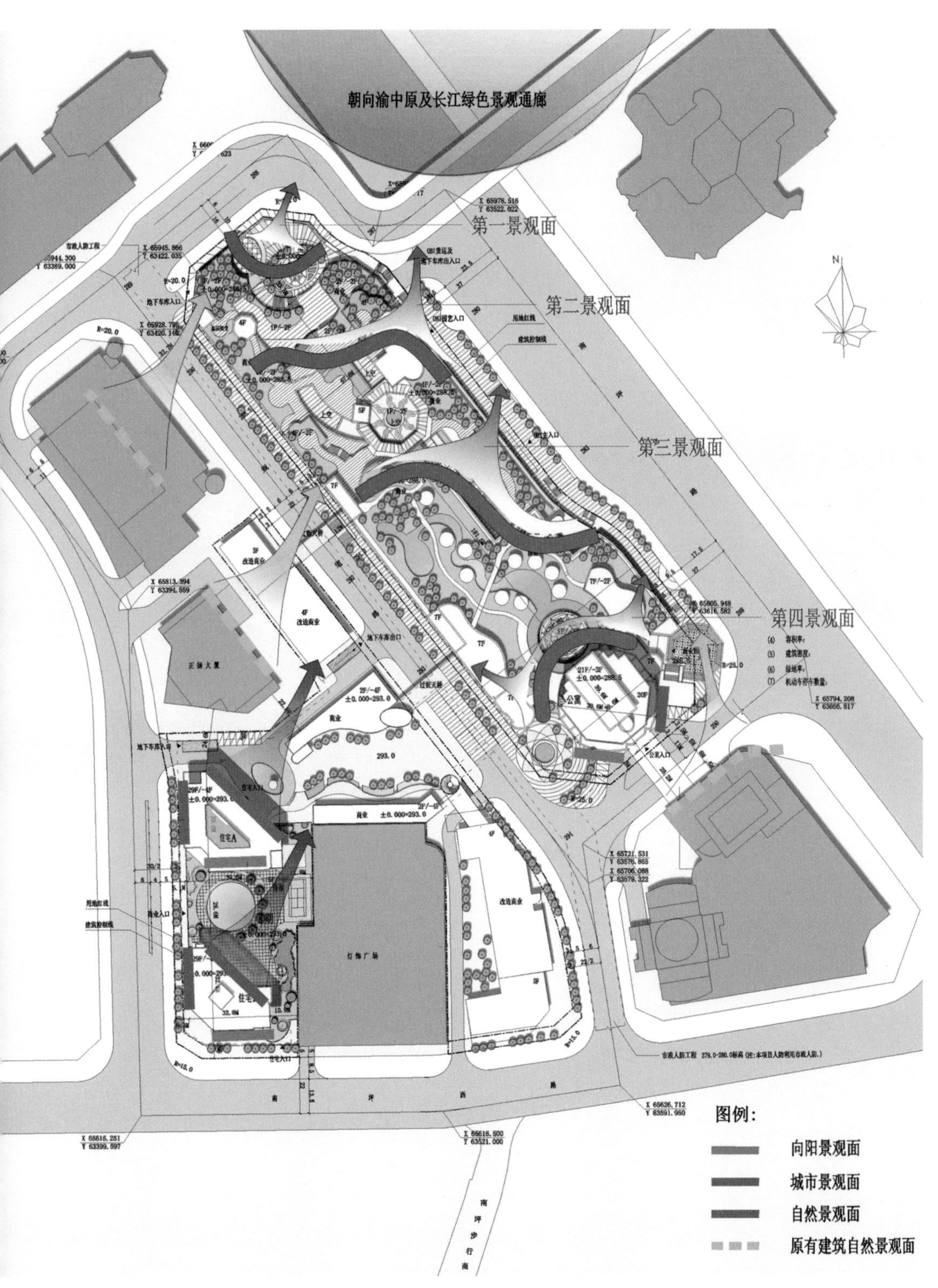

朝向渝中原及长江绿色景观通廊
第一景观面
第二景观面
第三景观面
第四景观面
正扬大厦
灯饰广场
改造商业
公寓
住宅A
商业
南坪西路
图例:
向阳景观面
城市景观面
自然景观面
原有建筑自然景观面

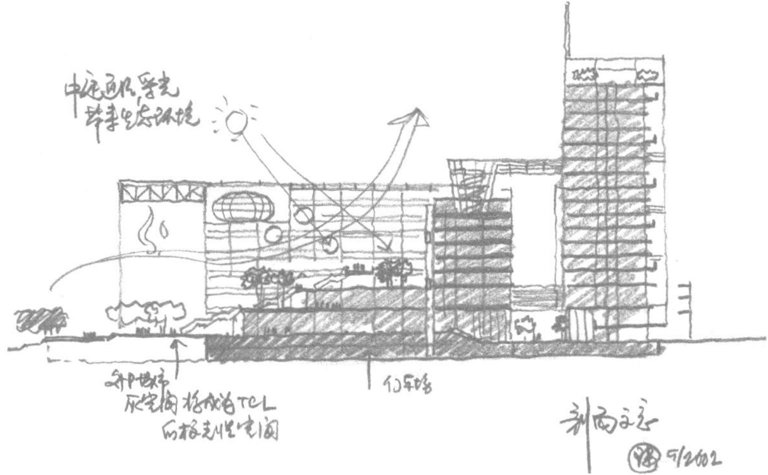

Project TCL Industrial Research
Location Shenzhen
Purpose offices
Area 78,102 m²
Design/Completion 2001/2004

Project Le Parc
Location Shenzhen
Purpose residential
Area 410,000 m²
Design/Completion 1999–2003/2003

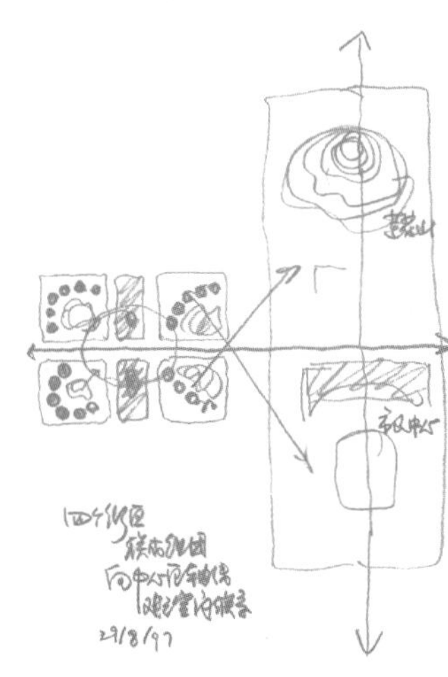
29/8/97

LA CIME INTERNATIONAL PTE LTD.

▼

Song Zhaoqing
Rong Rong
Ren Zhiguo
Yu Bo
Yin Xingyuan
Li Jie

▶ www.lacime-sh.com

This Shanghai-based firm began life in 1997 as a construction company with a planning department. Two years later it had received its licence as an architecture office. The company now employs over 30 architects, six leading design architects and nine project planners. Underpinning all of the firm's designs is the question of whether the planned building will be in harmony with its environs. Rational approaches come second to the issue of the human emotions that the architect wishes to evoke. This is because the poetry associated with the forms and materials of a particular location is apt to suffer during the process of grafting a western style of building onto the Chinese environment. In championing an »architecture of the poetic« the company owners are keen to combat the risk being posed to local architectural identities.

Das Büro mit Sitz in Shanghai begann 1997 zunächst als Baufirma mit Planungsabteilung und wurde zwei Jahre später als Architekturbüro anerkannt und registriert. Das Unternehmen beschäftigt heute mehr als 30 Architekten, sechs leitende Entwurfsarchitekten sowie neun Projektplaner. Das baukünstlerische Konzept, das den Ausgangspunkt aller Entwürfe des Büros bildet, geht immer der Frage nach, ob die geplante Architektur mit der Umgebung harmoniert. Dabei steht weniger der rationale Ansatz im Vordergrund als vielmehr die Frage nach den Emotionen, die von der jeweiligen Architektur evoziert werden. Denn mit der oft bedenkenlosen Adaptation westlicher Baustile geht auch eine Poesie des Ortes verloren, die an bestimmte Formen und Materialien gebunden war. Mit ihrer »Architektur des Poetischen« wollen die Inhaber des Büros diesem drohenden Verlust lokaler Identitäten entgegenwirken.

▲▶

Project East Lake Kindergarden, Suzhou Industrial Park | **Location** to the east of Jinji Lake, Suzhou Industrial Park
Purpose education | **Area** 2,000 m² | **Completion** 03.2004 | **Architect** Song Zhaoqing, Ren Zhiguo
Associate Architectural Design & Research Institute of Suzhou

▲▼
Project Shenzhen International Tennis Center
Location Xiangmi Lake, Shenzhen
Purpose sports, leisure, residential
Area 200,000 m^2
Completion 08.2004
Architect Song Zhaoqing, Ren Zhiguo, Gong Guan

▲
Project Shanghai Vision Trip
Location Shanghai Pudong SANLIN
Purpose residential, retail trade
Completion 10.2005
Architect Song Zhaoqing
Associate Shanghai JinDian Architectural & Planning PTELTD

Project Chongqing Jinxiu Mountain Garden
Location Renhe District, Chongqing
Purpose residential
Area 776 m²
Completion 12.2003
Architect Song Zhaoqing, Ren Zhiguo

Project Shenzhen Ocean World | **Location** Shekou District, Shenzhen | **Purpose** entertainment
Completion 12.2003 | **Architect** Song Zhaoqing, Ren Zhiguo, Gong Guan

UNIVERSAL ARCHITECTURE & ENGINEERING

Chen Xiangdong
Lin Jingsheng
He Zhong
Zhou Jianrong
Lu Jian
Wu Yanqin

www.uae.sh.cn

Founded in March 2002 this firm had its origins in the Shanghai Architectural Design Institute Co. Ltd. Besides architecture and landscape and interior design the practice provides consultation and planning services on engineering aspects including statics and domestic and supply engineering. The founders see the company focussing on a successful blend of solid architecture and modern technology, a combination that is increasingly sought after by today's building principals and end users. The proprietors of UA & E consider China's accession to the WTO to be a decisive step in the opening up of China to the outside world and in the modernisation of the country, which encompasses urban construction and architecture.

Das im März 2002 gegründete Büro ging aus dem Shanghai Architectural Design Institute Co. Ltd. hervor. Das Angebot umfasst neben Architektur, Landschaftsgestaltung und Innenarchitektur auch Beratungs- und Planungsleistungen im Ingenieurbereich; unter anderem Statik sowie Haus- und Versorgungstechnik. Ihren Schwerpunkt setzen die Gründer des Büros in der Verbindung von solider Architektur und moderner Technik, die den gestiegenen Ansprüchen der Bauherren und Nutzer entgegenkommt. Im Beitritt Chinas zur WTO sehen die Inhaber von UA & E einen entscheidenden Schritt zur Öffnung und Modernisierung des Landes auch im Bereich Städtebau und Architektur.

▲ ▶
Project Qingpu Museum
Location Qingpu District, Shanghai
Purpose museums
Area 8,000 m²
Design/Completion 2001/2004
Architect Xing Tonghe, Lin Jingsheng, Wu Yanqin, Gu Xinwei

The extraordinary shape echoes the scale and openness of the city and the ebullience of the local culture.
Die ungewöhnliche Form des Grundrisses soll die Offenheit und das überschäumende Wesen der Stadt Qingpu verkörpern.

▶ ▼

Project Shanghai Rivera Garden
Location 1898, Changning road, Changning District, Shanghai
Purpose residential
Area 88,100 m²
Design/Completion 2001/2004
Architect Lin Jingsheng, Wu Yanqin, Gu Xinwei

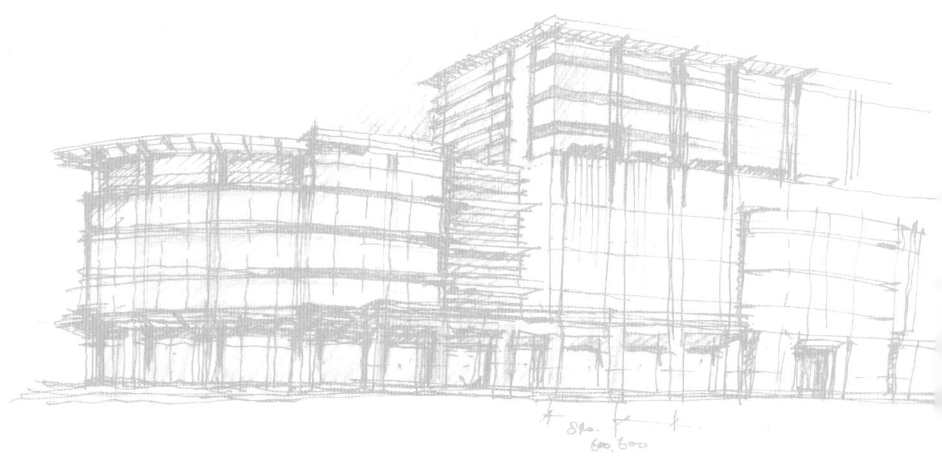

▲
Project Shanghai Huiheng Commercial Center
Location Caobao road. & Qixin road, Qibao, Shanghai
Purpose retail trade, offices
Area 65,000 m²
Design 2004
Architect Lin Jingsheng, Lu Jian, Wu Yanqin, Gu Xinwei

Project Shanghai South Chongqing road. 38-40-41 Plot Renovation Planning | **Location** South Chongqing road. 38-40-41 Plot
Purpose residential | **Area** 94,100 m² | **Design/Completion** 2003 | **Architect** Lin Jingsheng, Wu Yanqin, Gu Xinwei, Du Yuming

Project New Campus Taiyuan Normal University
Location Xiaodian Education Park, Taiyuan, Shanxi Province
Purpose education
Area 510,000 m²
Design 10.2005
Architect He Zhong, Lu Jian

HEY,
GATEWAY DELL
& MICRON
STREET WEAR

COBBLESTONE ARCHITECTURE + URBAN DESIGN WORKSHOP SHANGHAI

▼
Zumin Bian (Canada)
Tingjie(Peter) Liu
Adam Ho

▶ comerstone@online.sh.cn

This architecture practice based in Vancouver, Canada, and Shanghai represents a contemporary, innovative architecture that takes its inspiration from a number of different sources. Against a backdrop of constant change in the urban setting the company's architects are developing ideas for a physical order that is nonetheless ephemeral. Their designs are a kind of snapshot taken as the urban environment evolves around them. The somewhat theoretical definitions conceal a variety of projects in both China and Canada, all of which have taken careful account of their respective locations and cannot disguise the strong influence that western trends have had on the designs.

Das in Vancouver/Kanada und in Shanghai ansässige Büro steht für zeitgenössische, innovative Architektur, die von verschiedenen Einflüssen geprägt ist. Ausgehend von den ständigen Wandlungsprozessen im urbanen Kontext, entwickeln die Architekten Ideen für eine gleichwohl ephemere räumliche Ordnung. Die Entwürfe sind eine Art Momentaufnahme innerhalb der permanenten Evolution des städtischen Raums. Hinter den etwas theorielastigen Definitionen verbergen sich verschiedene Projekte sowohl in China als auch in Kanada, die mit Rücksicht auf ihre jeweilige Umgebung entstanden sind und ihre enge Verwandtschaft mit westlich-internationalen Trends nicht verhehlen können.

▲▶
Project New Shanghai International Convention Center Hotel and affiliated projects
Location Shanghai | **Purpose** hotel, commercial, offices, residential | **Area** 185,000 m² | **Design/Completion** 2004/2008

Urban mixture: hotel, apartments and offices
Urbaner Mix: Hotel, Wohnen und Büros

◄ ▼
Project Multi-Purpose Facility in Smartpark, University of Manitoba, Canada
Location University of Manitoba, Canada
Purpose Multi-Purpose Facility
Area 3,000 m^2
Design/Completion 2002/2003
Architect Tingjie (Peter) Liu, Ray Wan Architects

▲◄
Project Reconstruction of Renmin road
Location Taizhou, Jiangsu Province
Purpose residential
Area 122,352 m²
Design 2005
Architect Tingjie (Peter) Liu,
Ray Wan Architects

Reconstruction of an urban residential area
Rekonstruktion eines städtischen Wohnbereichs

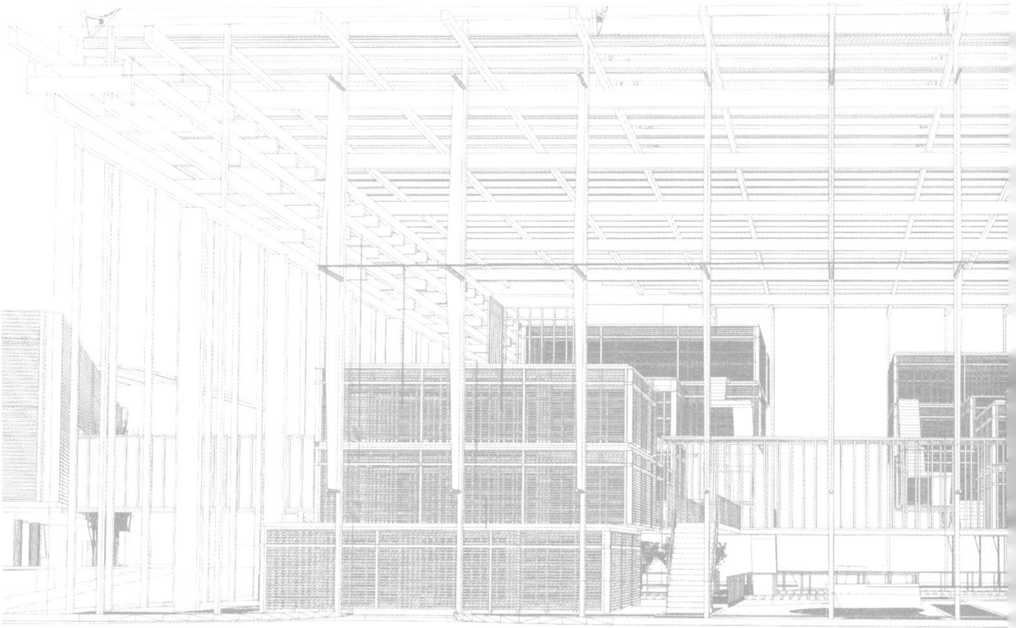

Project Chinese Artist Working/Living Studio
Location Winnipeg, Canada
Purpose office, residential
Area 10,000 m²
Design 2002

Inspired by Chinese traditions: studio for a Chinese artist, proposal

Inspiriert von chinesischen Bautraditionen: Entwurf für das Studio eines chinesischen Künstlers

PAN-PACIFIC DESIGN & DEVELOPMENT GROUP

▼

Zhang Hongwei
Chen Peiwen
Wang Weijin
Jin Chen
Huang Fang
Yu Ming
Feng Wei
Wang Xu Yuan
Cao Xingru

▶ www.ppddg.com

In opening an office in Shanghai this firm, founded in 1994 and based in Canada, has successfully made the leap into Asia. The Chinese branch, set up in 1995 and now employing a staff of 70, offers a full array of services covering architecture, urban planning and landscape and interior design. The company's experience of the roiling social and spatial upheavals going on in Shanghai have found expression in its own philosophy: the firm has nailed its colours to the mast of »green« architecture, which aims at minimal impact on the social environment and tries to meet the increasing demand for sustainable building projects and an ecological attitude to construction. This approach is not restricted to urban building designs but includes designs for commercial and office premises and public buildings.

Das in Kanada ansässige Büro, gegründet 1994, hat mit seinem Büro in Shanghai den Sprung nach Asien geschafft. Der 1995 eröffnete Ableger bietet mit Architektur, Stadtplanung, Landschaftsgestaltung und Innenarchitektur ein umfassendes Leistungsspektrum und beschäftigt derzeit 70 Mitarbeiter. In der Firmenphilosophie schlägt sich auch die Erfahrung des überschäumenden sozialen und räumlichen Wandels in Shanghai nieder: Geplant wird hier »grüne« Architektur, die mit Rücksicht auf den schützenswerten Lebensraum der Gesellschaft entsteht und den Anforderungen an Nachhaltigkeit und ökologisches Wirtschaften gerecht zu werden versucht. Es geht um lebenswerte Räume. Dieser Ansatz beschränkt sich nicht auf städtebauliche Entwürfe, sondern geht auch in die Entwürfe für Geschäfts- und Bürobauten oder öffentliche Gebäude ein.

▲
Project Science & Educational Center of Shanghai Tobacco Group Corp.
Location Changyang road, Shanghai
Purpose offices
Area 53,439 m²
Design 2002

▶ ▼
Project Five Ring Stadium
Location Changchun, Jilin Province
Purpose sports, leisure
Area 10,000 seats (8,000 fixed, 2,000 flexible)
Design/Completion 1994/1997
Associate Annau Architect Co. (Canada)

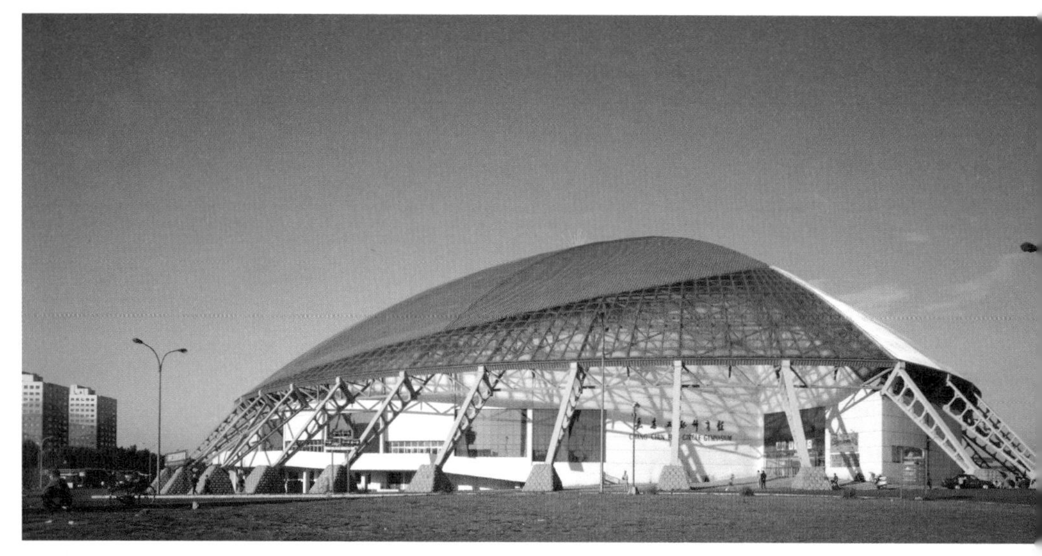

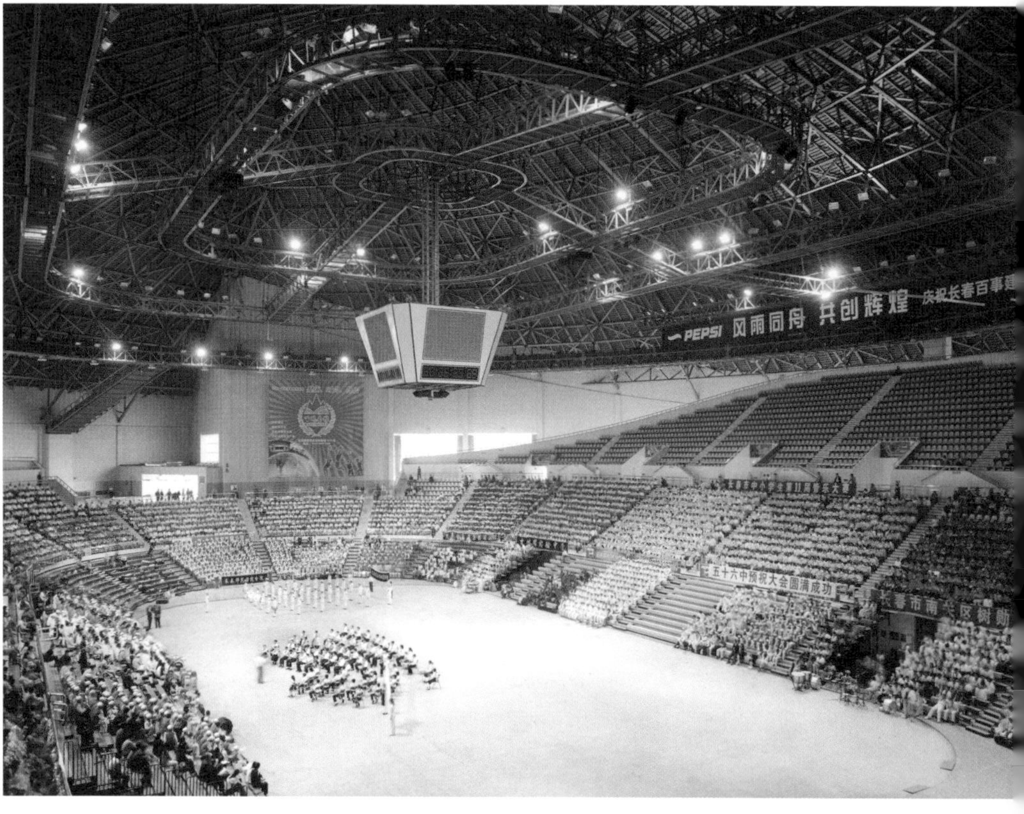
PEPSI 风雨同舟 共创辉煌
五十六中校庆大会圆满成功

▲◄
Project Changzhou Software Park
Location South Taihu road, Changzhou
Purpose offices
Area 26,500 m²
Design/Completion 2002/2004
Associate Annau Architect Co. (Canada)

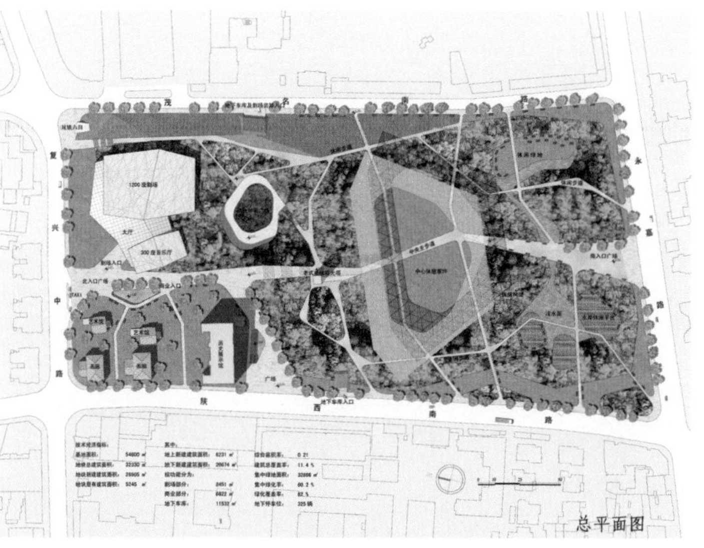

◄▼
Project Culture Plaza Redevelopment
Location 36 Yongjia road, Shanghai
Purpose landscape architecture
Area 32,330 m^2
Design 2004

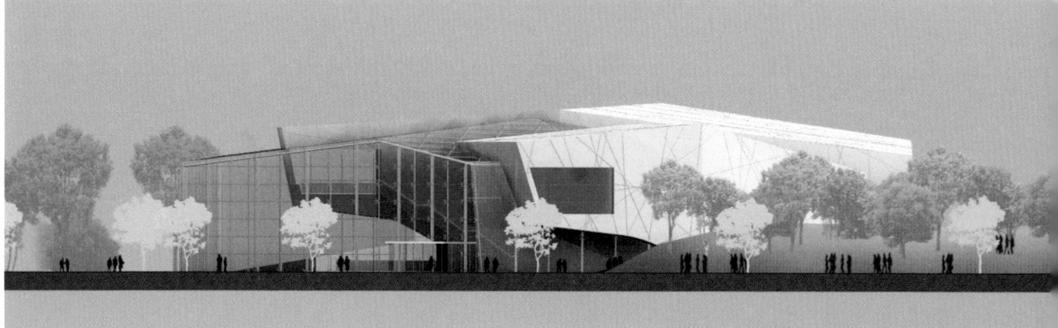

▲▼◄

Project The Bund District Functional Development and Comprehensive Traffic Planning
Location Shanghai
Purpose offices
Area 3.4 km²
Design 2004 (for competition)
Associate Shanghai Engineering Design Institute, Maunsell Consultants (Asia) Limited

ONE DESIGN

Bu Bing

Feng Ke

Qian Tongshen

▶ office@onedesigninc.com

This architecture firm registered in Shanghai and the USA sees itself as a bridge between east and west and is dedicated to maintaining a modern, international outlook. The company's young architects, most of whom have some form of international background, embrace diversity, both in their work and in modern architecture as a whole. The company's owners consider themselves not as experts in a given narrow field but rather as design specialists interested in using architecture to develop an identity for a particular location, town or street. The designs are always contextualised; the idea for a solution emerges in the course of studying the complex matrix of realities within which a building is to be created. Size is less important here than a fully-fledged grasp of the whole.

Das in Shanghai und den USA registrierte Büro versteht sich als west-östlicher Brückenschlag und hat sich konsequent einem modernen, internationalen Ansatz verschrieben. Den jungen Architekten, meist mit einem internationalen Hintergrund, geht es um die Vielfalt – sowohl im Hinblick auf ihre Arbeit als auch in Bezug auf moderne Architektur. So verstehen sich die Inhaber der Büros nicht als Fachspezialisten für eine bestimmte Bau- oder Projekttypologie, sondern als Entwurfsspezialisten, denen es darum geht, mithilfe von Architektur für einen bestimmten Ort, eine Stadt oder eine Straße eine Identität zu entwickeln. Die Entwürfe stehen immer in einem Kontext; die Idee für eine spezifische Lösung entsteht in der Auseinandersetzung mit der komplexen Realität, in der ein Bauwerk errichtet werden soll. Dabei geht es weniger um die Größe als um den jeweiligen Bezug zum Ganzen.

▲▶▼
Project Shanghai JD Tower
Location Shanghai
Purpose offices
Area 20,000 m²
Design/Completion 2004/2005
Architect Li Gang
Associate MAA Engineering Consultants (Shanghai) Co., Ltd.

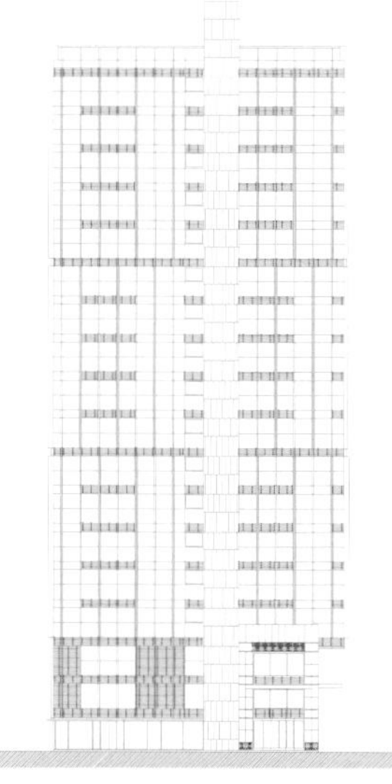

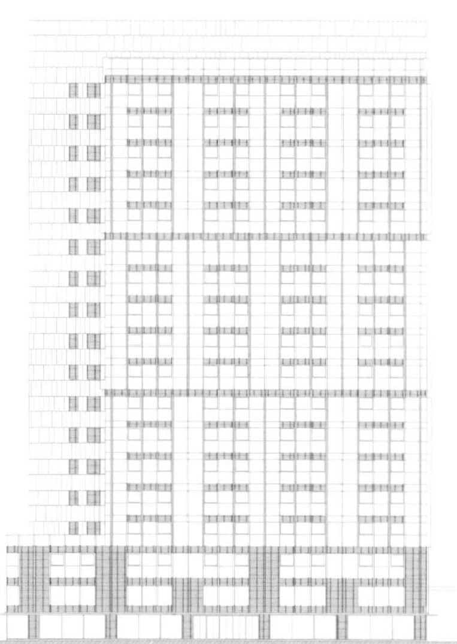

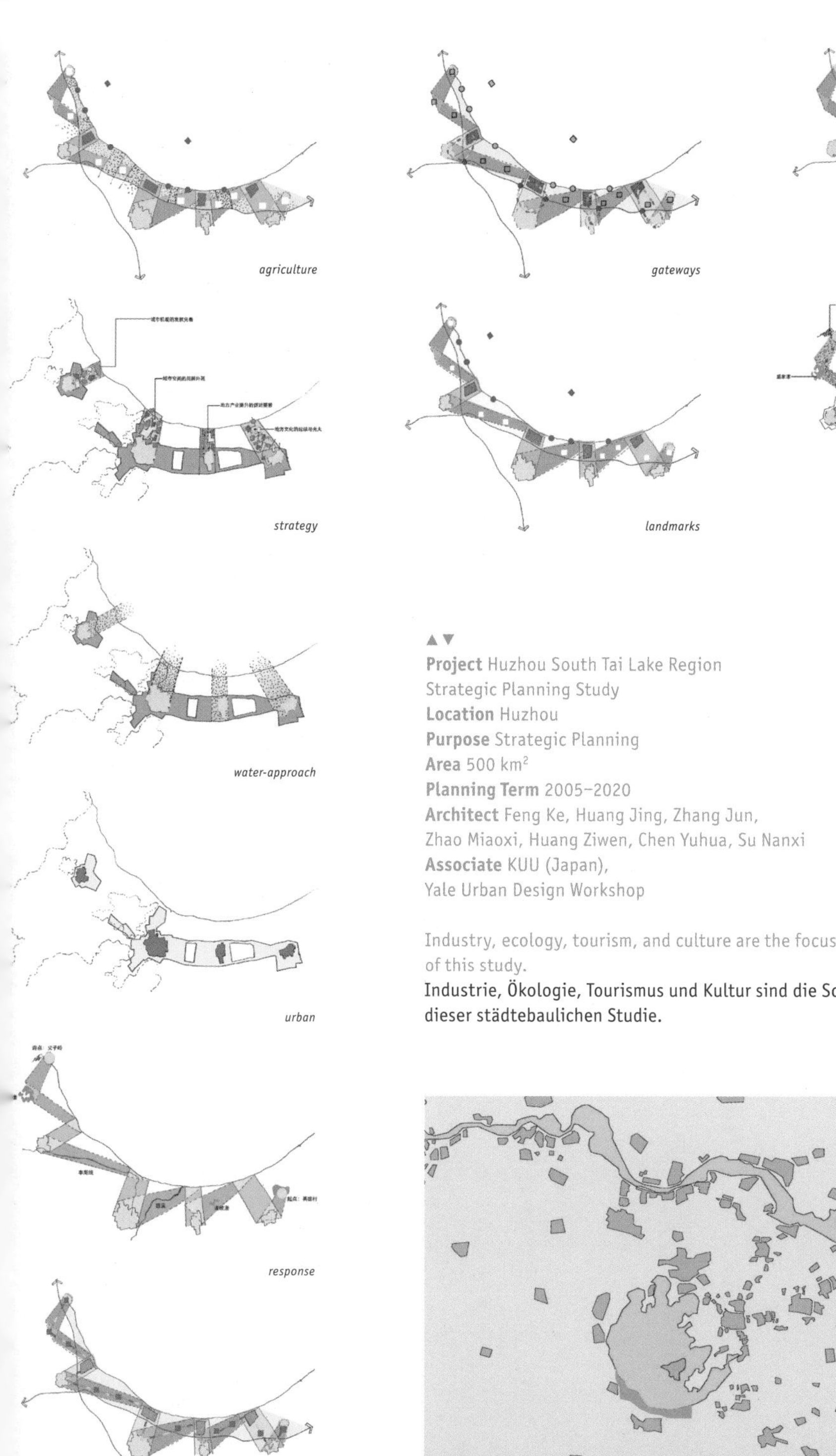

▲▼

Project Huzhou South Tai Lake Region
Strategic Planning Study
Location Huzhou
Purpose Strategic Planning
Area 500 km²
Planning Term 2005–2020
Architect Feng Ke, Huang Jing, Zhang Jun,
Zhao Miaoxi, Huang Ziwen, Chen Yuhua, Su Nanxi
Associate KUU (Japan),
Yale Urban Design Workshop

Industry, ecology, tourism, and culture are the focus points of this study.

Industrie, Ökologie, Tourismus und Kultur sind die Schwerpunkte dieser städtebaulichen Studie.

Project Ningbo Wulongtan Resort Hotel
Location Qingyunti, Wulongtan Tourist Area, Yinzhou District, Ningbo
Purpose hotel
Area 5,500 m²
Design/Completion 2003/2006
Architect Li Gang, Wang Yinghui, Zhang Xin
Associate Ningbo Institute of Civic Architectural Design & Research

Resort hotel in a scenic valley
Resort Hotel in einem malerischen Tal

PLAZA REAL
Coca-Cola
PLAZA REAL

SHANGHAI SUNYAT ARCHITECTURE DESIGN INSTITUTE

▼

Gao Dong
Lin Jun

▶ www.sunyat.com

This office had its beginnings in a planning institute established in 1984 and since 1996 has been designing residential and commercial premises for the Chinese market. Sunyat was one of the first companies in China to shift its status from public institute to commercial architecture practice. By setting up small design departments the company was able to retain a strong degree of control over its creative processes and operate relatively freely while its honed communications methods allow all planners to interact smoothly with one another. The eclectic architectural language and statements of the numerous completed projects reflect the many international influences flowing into the company's designs.

Das Büro ging aus einem 1984 gegründeten Planungsinstitut hervor und arbeitet seit 1996 als Anbieter von Geschäfts- und Wohnbauarchitektur auf dem chinesischen Markt. Die Umstellung von einem staatlichen Institut hin zu einem kommerziellen Architekturbüro vollzog Sunyat als eine der ersten Firmen in China. Mit der Schaffung kleiner Entwurfs-Abteilungen gelang es, den kreativen Prozess relativ unabhängig und frei von Routineabläufen zu gestalten; während die Nutzung ausgefeilter Kommunikationstechniken alle Planungsbeteiligten in die Lage versetzt, ohne Hindernisse miteinander zu kommunizieren. Die eklektische Architektursprache der zahlreichen realisierten Projekte spiegelt die vielen internationalen Einflüsse wider, die in die Entwürfe des Büros eingehen.

▲▶

Project Chenghuang Temple Plaza, Yuyuan Garden
Location Middle Fangbang road, Huang Pu District, Shanghai
Purpose commercial, retail trade | **Area** 35,000 m²
Design 2004 | **Architect** Lin Jun, Zheng Yan

 This project preserves the character and traditions of the old Yuyuan Garden area.
 In diesem Projekt wurde der traditionelle Charakter der historischen Gartenlandschaft von Yuyuan bewahrt.

Project Blue Cambridge
Location Xin Song road, Song Jiang New Town
Purpose residential
Area 68,000 m^2
Design/Completion 2004/2005
Architect Gao Dong, Zhu Yumei, Wang Fang

Project Hong Qiao East Garden
Location Hongxin road, Minhang District
Purpose residential | **Area** 180,000 m²
Design/Completion 2003/2005
Architect Gao Dong, Zhu Yumei

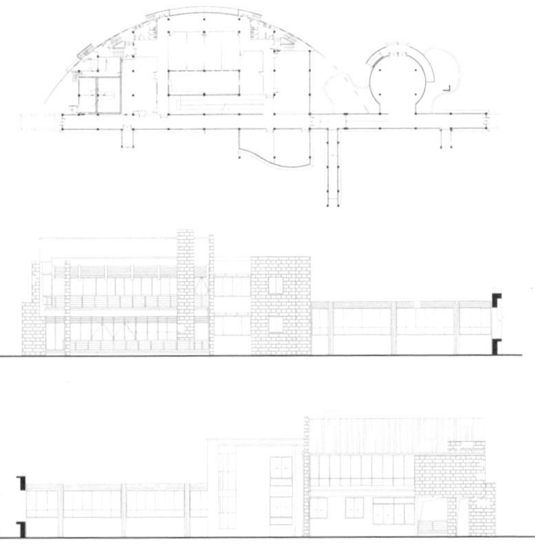

Project Tianma Hill Branch of Zhongshan Hospital
Location Southern foot of Tianma Hill, Sheshan Mountain, Songjiang National Tourist Park, Shanghai
Purpose hospital
Area 10,000 m²
Design/Completion 2003/2004
Architect Ke Jianglin, Zhu Yumei

Harmony between architecture and environment
Harmonie zwischen Architektur und belebter Welt

9-TOWN DESIGN STUDIO FOR URBAN ARCHITECTURE

▼

Zhang Yingpeng

Yu Lei

Chen Yong

▶ www.9-town.com

This office, whose staff includes three architects with doctorates and many engineering and planning graduates, is committed to maintaining a narrow link between scientific research and architectural practice. Its designs and projects reveal a strong desire to explore the nature of architecture – on the one hand as art and on the other hand as a practical solution to building needs. This tension forms the seedbed from which the young architects, all graduates of Southeast University, go about planning their projects. International influences are as crucial here as technical innovations and the new possibilities presented to a society in the process of opening up to the outside world.

Das Büro, in dem neben drei promovierten Architekten auch diplomierte Ingenieure und Fachplaner beschäftigt sind, steht für eine enge Verbindung von wissenschaftlicher Forschung und architektonischer Praxis. Ihre Entwürfe und Projekte zeugen von der gründlichen Auseinandersetzung mit Architektur als Kunst einerseits und praktischer Lösung andererseits. In diesem akademisch ausgeloteten Spannungsverhältnis entwickeln die jungen Architekten, allesamt Absolventen der Southeast University, ihre Planungen. Internationale Einflüsse spielen dabei eine ebenso große Rolle wie technische Innovationen und die neuen Möglichkeiten einer sich öffnenden Gesellschaft.

▲
Project Nanyang College, (phase II), Wuxi | **Location** Taihu vacation district, Wuxi
Purpose education, offices | **Area** 58,000 m²
Design/Completion 10.2001/08.2002 | **Architect** Zhang Yingpeng, Shen Qiming

▶
Project Interior Design of 9-town Design Studio for Urban Architecture
Location F9, Guoji Square, No. 200, Xinghai street | **Purpose** offices
Area 500 m² | **Design/Completion** 10.2004/12.2004 | **Architect** Zhang Yingpeng

The expressive use of primary colors conveys the creativity of the design company.
Charakteristisch für das Büro ist die Verwendung ausdrucksstarker, leuchtender Farben.

Project Youth Community, Suzhou Industrial Park
Location Xinglong street and Zhongyuan road, Suzhou Industrial Park
Purpose residential, offices
Area 247,060 m^2 (phase 1), 95,095 m^2 (phase 2)
Design/Completion 09.2002/12.2004
Architect Chengyong, Zhu Xiaochun, Zhang Yingpeng

HEY,
GATEWAY, DELL
& MICRON...

◀
Project Commercial Center, Block 51306, Loufeng County, Suzhou Industrial Park
Location east of Xinghu street and north of Dongjing road
Purpose commercial
Area 53,113 m² | **Design** 06.2005
Architect Yu Lei, Jiang Lei, Shen Qiming

▶
Project East Lakeside Neighbourhood Center, Suzhou Industrial Park
Location south of Zhongyuan road, east of Xinglong street
Purpose offices, restaurant, retail trade
Area 25,000 m² | **Design** 04.2005
Architect Yu Lei, Shen Qiming

HAIPO ARCHITECTS

Wu Haiqing

Chen Libo

▶ www.hpa.cn

The company was founded back in 1993 by two architects who returned to China after a decade spent gathering professional experience in the USA. The two offices, one in Beijing, one in Shanghai, now employ more than 100 people including architects from Germany and the USA. The office is involved in almost all forms of construction, from residential buildings and commercial premises to public institutions, leisure centres and urban planning projects. At HAIPO architecture is regarded as a »practical art« that can only be described as successful if it responds to the needs of the user, the relevant environment and ecological determinants. Architectural innovation comes from changes in the everyday lives of people, in their needs and desires.

Das Büro gibt es bereits seit 1993. Gegründet wurde es von zwei Architekten, die nach gut zehn Jahren Berufserfahrung in den USA nach China zurückkehrten. In den zwei Büros in Peking und Shanghai sind mittlerweile über 100 Mitarbeiter beschäftigt, darunter auch Architekten aus Deutschland und den USA. Das Leistungsspektrum umfasst nahezu alle Bautypologien – von Wohn- und Geschäftsbauten über öffentliche Einrichtungen und Freizeitanlagen bis hin zu Stadtplanung. Architektur wird als »praktische Kunst« betrachtet, die nur dann als erfolgreich und gelungen bezeichnet werden kann, wenn sie den Bedürfnissen der Nutzer, der jeweiligen Umgebung sowie ökologischen Maßgaben gerecht wird. Architektonische Innovation ergibt sich aus den Veränderungen des Alltags der Menschen, ihrer Bedürfnisse und Ansprüche.

▲▲
◄▼
Project Shanghai Silver City Cyber Tower
Location No. 75, Guangdong road, Shanghai
Purpose offices | **Area** 64,680 m^2
Design/Completion 1999/2002
Architect Chen Libo, Chen Weifang, Jia Nan

Landmark on the Shanghai Skyline: Silver City Cyber Tower
Landmarke der Skyline von Shanghai: der Silver City Cyber Tower

Project Shanghai Royal Garden
Location Gudai road, Minhang District, Shanghai
Purpose residential
Area 430,100 m²
Design/Completion 1998/2002
Architect Cheng Libo, Qian Wenjun, Li Xieming, Tang Min

Project Shanghai Electric Tower
Location Century street, Pudong, Shanghai
Purpose offices
Area 62,108 m^2
Design/Completion 2001/2004
Architect Wu Haiqing, Xiao Nan, Zhu Hong, Yang Weifang, Gao Yimei

The 30-storey tower is a mixture of a naval flagship with futuristic sci-fi flair.
Das Äußere des 30-geschossigen Glasturms ist eine Mischung aus maritimen und futuristischen Elementen.

JIANGNAN ARCHITECTURE DESIGN INSTITUTE

Gu Yucheng
Xiang Yin
Shi Jianliang
Zou Wei
Huang Jianbing
Ren Jian
Wang Lihua
Lin Yonghong
Song Hebin
Jiang Bing
Ruan Yaohua
Liu Xiaorong
Wang Zili

▶ www.jnadi.com

This architecture firm had its beginnings in the Jiading planning institute in Shanghai. The company, which is fully subject to market forces, employs more than 180 people including numerous specialised planners and engineers. Many of them can boast considerable experience and a very thorough knowledge of Chinese architecture circles. These skills are what have earned the company its reputation, especially in the region of Jiangnang. Traditions peculiar to this area at the lower reaches of the Yangtse River have always been reflected in the designs and buildings of the company. The planning process has always been informed by the cultural specificities of the region and at the same time has incorporated technological and architectural innovations.

Das aus dem Jiading Planungsinstitut Shanghai hervorgegangene marktwirtschaftlich organisierte Unternehmen beschäftigt mehr als 180 Mitarbeiter; darunter auch zahlreiche Fachplaner und Ingenieure. Viele davon können auf eine lange Berufserfahrung zurückblicken und besitzen sehr gründliche Kenntnisse der chinesischen Architekturszene. Diese Kompetenzen begründen auch den guten Ruf des Büros, das sich vor allem in der Region Jiangnan einen Namen gemacht hat. Die spezifischen Traditionen dieser Gegend am unteren Lauf des Yangtse-Flusses sind von jeher in die Entwürfe und Bauten des Büros eingegangen. So erfolgt der Planungsprozess immer mit Rücksicht auf die regionalen kulturellen Besonderheiten und integriert gleichzeitig technische wie auch architektonische Innovationen.

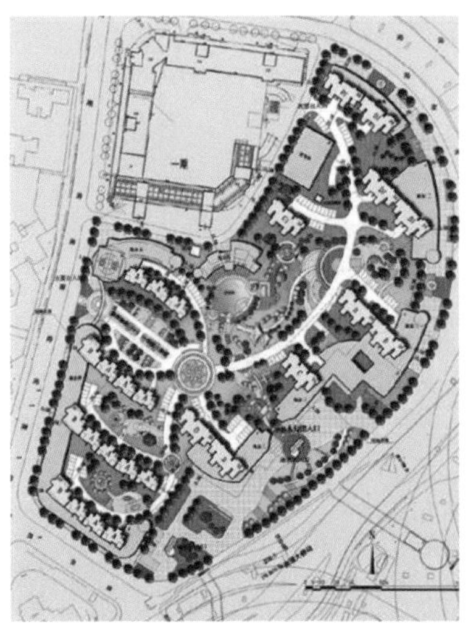

▲◀
Project Zhong Fu Garden
Location Shanghai
Purpose residential
Area 216,390 m²
Design 2003
Architect Gu Yucheng, Ren Jian, Luan Yaohua

Project The Government Office in Jia Ding | **Location** Jia Ding, Shanghai
Purpose offices | **Area** 97,400 m²
Design/Completion 1996/05.1998
Architect Gu Yucheng, Ren Jian, Song Hebin

Project Elysee Garden | **Location** Ye Cheng road, Jia Ding
Purpose residential | **Area** 150,000 m² | **Design/Completion** 2002/2003
Architect Song Hebin, Wang Kuixing, Xu Lei

▲▶
Project Jin Di Ge Lin Garden
Location Xi Men, Jia Ding
Purpose residential
Area 170,000 m^2
Design/Completion 2003/2004
Architect Jin Jun, Xu Lei

GOM DESIGN INTERNATIONAL

Zhang Jiajing

▶ www.gom.com.cn

This successful company, founded in Shanghai in 1997, opened a branch in Chicago, USA, in 2004. With no more than a dozen employees GOM pursues a strategy borrowed from the Chinese game »Go«, whence the firm takes its name. The company is preoccupied less with short-term profits than with long-term potential, less with short-lived interests than with sustainable developments. The architects' approach to designs is one of a realistic pragmatism that rejects formal justifications, theory-bound derivatives and the intellectualism of aesthetic contortions. Yet despite their gravitas the architects follow a quasi-romantic ideal and create truly idyllic buildings. They could well be described as being the link between realism and the Romantic school.

Das erfolgreiche, 1997 in Shanghai gegründete Büro eröffnete 2004 auch einen Ableger in Chicago, USA. Mit gerade einem Dutzend Mitarbeitern verfolgt das Unternehmen eine Strategie, die dem chinesischen Spiel »Go« entlehnt ist, was wiederum auch in dem Namen des Büros zu finden ist. Dabei geht es weniger um kurzfristige Profite als um langfristige Potenziale, mehr um nachhaltige Entwicklungen und nicht um kurzlebige Interessen. Der Entwurfsansatz basiert auf einer Art realistischem Pragmatismus, dem intellektuell-ästhetische Verrenkungen ebenso fern liegen wie formale Rechtfertigungen oder theoretische Ableitungen. Doch trotz ihres nüchternen Selbstverständnisses verfolgen die Architekten ein fast romantisches Ideal und schaffen Räume, die durchaus idyllischen Charakter haben. Man könnte sie auch als Verbindung zwischen Realismus und Romantik verstehen.

▲▲
◀
Project Shanghai Waigaoqiao Port Inner Lateral Pier, Shanghai (phase V)
Location Gangjian road, Waigaoqiao Port, Shanghai
Purpose offices
Area 21,000 m²
Design/Completion 2004/2005
Architect Zhang Jiajing, Li Fengliang, Wu Jia
Partner Zhongyuan International Project Design Research Institute (Shanghai)

◄ ▼
Project Shanghai Sanxin Garden
Location Kangding road and Wanhangdu road, Shanghai
Purpose Residential and public facilities
Area 53,000 m^2
Design/Completion 1997/2005
Architect Zhang Jiajing, Jiang Lihang, Ma Jie, Liu Zeming, Kong Shaokai
Partner China Light Industry Design Research Institute, Shanghai

Project Beijing Seine-Villa
Location north of Lishui Bridge, Chaoyang District, Beijing
Purpose residential
Area 69,000 m^2
Design/Completion 2000/2001
Architect Jiajing Zhang, Hong Zhang
Partner Tsinghua Architectural Design Research Institute

走近
民間藝術
大师展

TIANJIN HUAHUI ARCHITECTURAL DESIGN AND ENGINEERING

▶ shtwdcadp@china.com

The ethos of this company created in Tianjin in 1995 can be found in its holistic approach to planning and design, an approach that combines rational and quasi-spiritual elements. The architects see it as their task to find the right type of architecture for each respective location and to show respect for the urban and natural surroundings while at the same time taking the economic imperatives of the market into consideration. Discussions at the design stage are less concerned with formal innovation than with the physical form best suited to the relevant location. Besides its standard architectural activities the company is also involved in urban planning and landscape and interior design. The company can already point to numerous completed projects across the country.

Das Selbstverständnis des 1995 in Tianjin gegründeten Unternehmens basiert auf einem ganzheitlichen Planungs- und Entwurfsansatz, der rationale Elemente ebenso wie quasi spirituelle Aspekte vereint. Den Architekten geht es darum, für den jeweiligen Ort eine optimale Architektur zu entwickeln, gleichwohl mit Respekt vor der städtischen Umgebung und der Natur, aber auch mit Blick auf die ökonomischen Erfordernisse des Marktes. Die Diskussion innerhalb des Entwurfsprozesses dreht sich weniger um formale Innovationen als vielmehr um die adäquate, am besten geeignete Form für den jeweiligen Standort. Neben den üblichen Architekturleistungen gehören auch Stadtplanung, Landschaftsgestaltung sowie Innenarchitektur zum Angebot des Büros, das bereits auf zahlreiche realisierte Projekte im ganzen Land verweisen kann.

▲ ▶ ▼

Project Feng Ji-cai Literature and Arts Research Institute, Tianjin University
Location Tianjin University
Purpose education
Area 6,000 m²
Design/Completion 2001/2004

Project Songshan Lake Library, Dongguan
Location Central Songshan Lake Scientific and Technological Industry Park
Purpose library | **Area** 15,000 m² | **Design/Completion** 2002/04.2003

Project MBA Central Building, Nankai University
Location Nankai University
(to the east of Baidi road, Nankai district, Tianjin)
Purpose education
Area 29,000 m²
Design/Completion 2001/04.2003

DDB INTERNATIONAL SHANGHAI

Xiang Bingren

▶ xiangbr@public3.sta.net.cn

Set up in 1998, this office, with its head offices in the port of Shanghai, is a branch of DDB International Hong Kong. The entrusting of the company's management to a famous architect with a decidedly academic background is clear evidence of the complexity of approach that is characteristic of all its designs. That architecture should also produce landmarks is evinced in particular by the company's spectacular office skyscrapers and the shell-shaped theatre in Hefei, Anhui Province. While it is projects like these that reflect the country's leanings to an international modernist style the villas and residential buildings are oriented towards the American ideal. Yet the company also pays homage to Chinese culture, as witnessed in its design for a cultural centre in Datang which includes traditional forms common in prestigious Chinese architecture.

Das Büro mit Sitz in der Hafenmetropole ist eine Filiale der DDB International Hongkong und wurde 1998 eröffnet. Dass die Leitung des Büros einem renommierten Architekten mit dezidiert akademischen Hintergrund angetragen wurde, beweist nicht zuletzt der komplexe Ansatz, der alle Entwürfe kennzeichnet. Architektur muss auch als Landmarke funktionieren, dies beweist DDB International vor allem mit den spektakulären Bürotürmen sowie dem muschelartigen Theaterbau von Hefei in der Provinz Anhui. Während diese Projekte die Hinwendung zur internationalen Moderne widerspiegeln, orientieren sich die Villen- und Wohnbauten am amerikanischen Ideal. Doch auch die Verbundenheit zur chinesischen Kultur wird in den Entwürfen gewürdigt. So fanden traditionelle Formen chinesischer Repräsentationsarchitektur Eingang in den Entwurf für ein Kulturzentrum in Datang.

▲ ▶

Project Reservation and renovation of West Lake Historic District
Location Hangzhou | **Purpose** residential | **Area** 35,467 m² | **Design** 2005

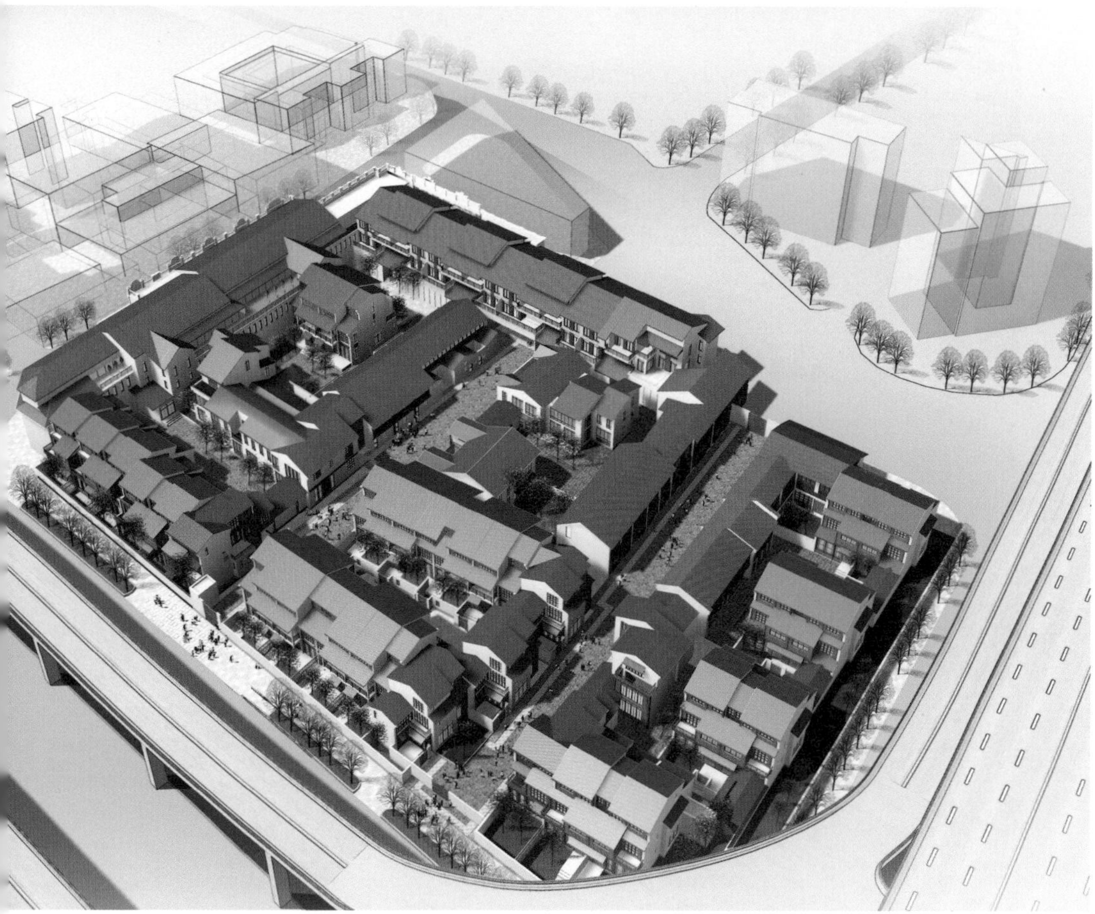

Project Hefei Grand Theatre
Location Hefei, Anhui Province
Purpose culture
Area 54,755 m^2
Design 2004
Architect Xiang Bingren, Qin Gejin, Miao Qi
Associate Tongji University Architectural Design and Research Institute

Project The Performing and Art Center of Datang Everbright Town
Location Xi'an | **Purpose** Performing and Art Center
Area 52,700 m^2 | **Design** 2006 | **Architect** Xiang Bingren, Chen Qiang

◀ ▼

Project Jingsha Site Museum
Location Chengdu
Purpose museum
Area 20,000 m^2
Design 2005
Architect Xiang Bingren, Wu Xin, Dong Yi

N. W. ARCHITECTURE DESIGN

▼

Guo Xuhui
Zhou Dongguang
Bao Zheng
Dong Chenghua
Lu Panfeng

This firm, founded in 1996, was one of the first architecture practices in China to receive a licence to operate on the private market. Today it employs more than 150 people. The company is involved in a wide spectrum of activities ranging from urban planning and building design to landscape planning and interior design. In spite of the undeniable influence of the international modern style the company relies to a large extent on traditional Chinese forms and building materials. The contemporary buildings include references to local and regional architecture, giving them a charm that anchors them firmly in their cultural environment. The villas and smaller public buildings are a delicate antidote to the many buildings serving as triumphal gestures of China's new power and can be said to embody the alternative side of contemporary Chinese architecture.

Das 1996 gegründete Büro gehörte zu den ersten staatlich anerkannten privatwirtschaftlichen Architekturunternehmen Chinas. Heute sind hier mehr als 150 Mitarbeiter beschäftigt. Das Angebotsspektrum des Büros reicht von Stadtplanung über Architektur bis hin zu Landschaftsplanung und Innenarchitektur. Trotz deutlicher Anleihen bei der internationalen Moderne setzt das Büro auch auf traditionelle chinesische Formen und Materialien. Gerade der Bezug auf lokale und regional spezifische Architektur verleiht den zeitgenössischen Bauten einen Charakter, der sie vor Beliebigkeit und Ortlosigkeit bewahrt. Während viele Bauten für staatliche Institutionen die Triumphgeste des erstarkenden und machtvollen Chinas widerspiegeln, wirken die Villenbauten oder kleinere öffentlichen Anlagen eher zierlich und verkörpern sozusagen die andere Seite der chinesischen Gegenwartsarchitektur.

▲▶

Project Tsinghua Tongfang Info Port
Location Lot D19, CBD, Hunnan Economy and Technology Development District, Shenyang | **Purpose** commercial | **Area** 270,000 m²

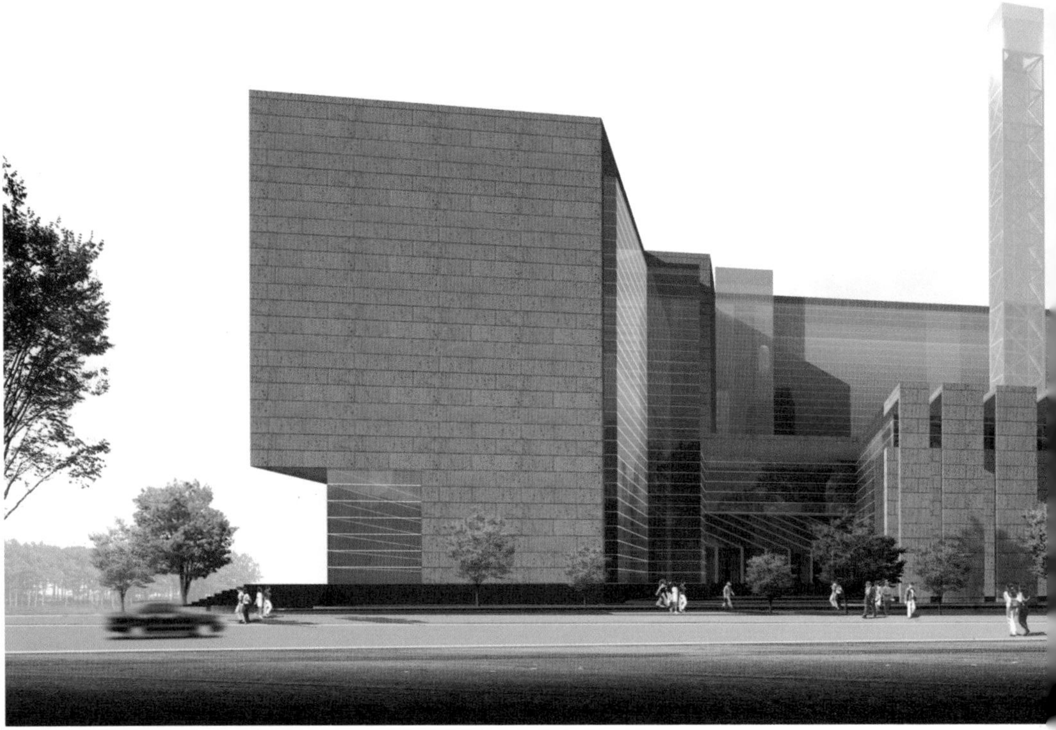

Project New Customs Building
Location Lot 13, CBD,
Hunnan New District, Shenyang
Purpose offices
Area 342,000 m²

Project Northeast China Yucai School Campus
Location Shenyang High and New Agricultural Technology Development District
Purpose education
Area 90,000 m^2
Design/Completion 2004/2005

上海湾 鄂尔多斯国际广场
LOEWE

NIKKO ARCHITECTURE CONSULTATION

▼
Wang Xingtian
Du Fuchun
Zhang Wenyu
Zhang Jun

▶ nikko@online.sh.cn

This company, founded in Shanghai in 1995 as a Chinese branch of the Japanese architecture firm »Four Doors & First Level«, has already brought to term more than 200 projects in the area of town planning and architecture. Besides landscape planning the company also offers interior design and environmental planning. The company's philosophy is based on a concept that sees Chinese architecture as revolving around centuries of traditions, forms and significances handed down over a period of centuries, with the associated »fringe« seen as a canvas on which a number of variations, interpretations and innovations can find expression. Nonetheless it is on the fringe that social and cultural change is most visible, more so than at the central axis, which is slower to reflect transformation and does so only in filtered form. As such the company aims at an architecture that admits a measure of social and aesthetic change while retaining its respect for the canon of Chinese architectural traditions.

Das Unternehmen, 1995 als chinesischer Ableger des japanischen Architekturbüros »Four Doors & First Level« in Shanghai gegründet, hat bereits mehr als 200 Projekte im Bereich Städtebau und Architektur realisiert. Zum Leistungsspektrum der Firma gehören neben Landschaftsplanung auch Innenarchitektur und Umweltplanung. Die Unternehmensphilosophie des Büros geht von einem Architekturverständnis aus, das im »Zentrum« des baukünstlerischen Schaffens die über Jahrhunderte weitergegebenen Traditionen, Formen und Bedeutungen sieht, während die damit zusammenhängende »Peripherie« als Spielfeld verstanden wird, auf dem Variationen, Interpretationen und Innovationen möglich sind. Gleichwohl werden in der »Peripherie« soziale und kulturelle Veränderungen schneller sichtbar als im »Zentrum«, das Wandel nur allmählich und vermittelt reflektiert. In diesem Verständnis strebt das Büro nach einer Architektur, die sich den sozialen und ästhetischen Veränderungen nicht verschließt, aber auch Respekt vor den kanonisierten Traditionen widerspiegelt.

MOULIN ROUGE-TRUTH
ROUGE-TRUTH
MOULIN ROUGE-TRUTH
MOULIN ROUGE
DIKENI
LANCOME

▲▲
▼

Project World Square
Location Shanghai
Purpose offices, commercial
Area 63,489 m²
Design/Completion 2002/2006

▲
Project Senior Citizen College and Entertainment Center, Wuxi | **Location** Wuxi, Jiangsu Province
Purpose education, leisure | **Area** 28,525 m^2 | **Design** 2005

Project Nantong Abacus Museum
Location Nantong, Jiangsu Province
Purpose museum
Area 5,100 m^2
Design/Completion 2002/2004

HUNAN QIANFU URBAN DESIGN

Zhang Nan

Cai Yongdong

▶ chief.www@263.net

This office was a scion of the former Institute for Urban Planning at Hunan University. Created in 2000, the company provides town planning services and also architectural design, open space planning and interior decoration. The office now employs over 70 people, many of whom have achieved high academic qualifications. The office is sensitive to trends, follows competent market strategies and conducts projects to consistently high standards. The subtle influence of modern western architecture, especially in leisure facility projects, is just as discernible as the firm's predilection for American-style residential blocks and the European style of villas and detached townhouses.

Das Büro ging im Jahr 2000 aus dem ehemaligen Institut für Städtebau der traditionsreichen Hunan Universität hervor und bietet neben städtebaulichen Leistungen auch Architektur, Freiraumplanung sowie Innenausstattung an. Es beschäftigt heute mehr als 70 Mitarbeiter; viele davon verfügen über einen ausgewiesenen akademischen Hintergrund. Sensibilität für Trends, kompetente Marktstrategien und eine hohe Qualität der Projekte zeichnen die Arbeit des Büros aus. Die sanften Anleihen bei westlicher moderner Architektur, vor allem im Bereich der Freizeitbauten, sind ebenso unübersehbar wie die Vorliebe für amerikanisch geprägte Wohnhäuser und den europäischen Villenstil.

▲ ▶
Project Tong Shenghu Villa
Location Changsha, Hunan | **Purpose** residential
Area 223,553 m^2 | **Architect** Cai Yongdong

European and American-style villas along Xiangjiang river in Hunan.
Wohnhäuser im amerikanischen und europäischen Stil am Xiangjiang Fluss in Hunan.

»On the tip of Orange Island/
The Xiang flowing northward/
I see a thousand hills crimsoned through ...«

Project The Xiang flowing northward:
Conceptual Design of Xiangjiang River Tourists Harbour
Location Changsha, Hunan
Purpose tourism, recreation
Area 15,653 m²
Architect Cai Yongdong

Project Youths Activities Center in Taoyuan Town
Location Taoyuan Town, Changde, Hunan Province
Area 4,086 m²
Architect Peng Qinfeng, Xiehui, Zhangyong, Luo Guchun

▲
Project Museum of ChengTou Mount Antiquity City
Location Li Town, Changde, Hunan Province
Area 3,468 m^2
Architect Zhangnan, Lu Jiansong, Luoyu

SHOPING

GREENTON ARCHITECTURAL DESIGN

▼
Wu Xiaoming
Zhu Qiulong
Yang Ming
Jiangyu
Wang Yuhong
Huang Yunian
Zhang Wei

▶ www.greentondesign.com

Founded in 1997, this office was one of the first architecture studios to pursue a narrow relationship with real estate companies and to gear itself closely to the market. Success has borne out the founders' strategy. Cooperation with real estate firms has had an advantageous effect on staff numbers and also led to a series of residential and commercial construction projects that not only take their lead from economic indicators but can also lay claim to a degree of architectural quality. The office is less concerned with creating its own unmistakeable signature than it is with its ability to respond in a variety of ways to the complex demands posed by a booming region. The influence of international trends in architecture can be clearly seen in the company's work.

Das 1997 gegründete Büro ist eines der ersten Architekturstudios, die eine enge Kooperation mit Immobilienunternehmen angestrebt haben und sich in ihrer Arbeit stark am Marktgeschehen orientieren. Der Erfolg gibt den Gründern des Büros recht. Die Zusammenarbeit mit Immobilienfirmen hat sich vorteilhaft auf die Entwicklung der Mitarbeiterzahl ausgewirkt und auch dazu geführt, dass der Wohnungs- und Geschäftsbau nicht nur wirtschaftlichen Maßstäben folgt, sondern auch eine architektonische Qualität für sich beanspruchen kann. Das Büro legt weniger Wert auf eine unverwechselbare Handschrift als vielmehr auf die Fähigkeit, mit verschiedenen Ansätzen auf die komplexen Aufgaben in einer Wachstumsregion zu reagieren. Der Bezug auf internationale Architekturtrends ist dabei unübersehbar.

▲ ▶

Project Wealth Center

Location Ningbo | **Purpose** residential | **Area** 60,000 m² | **Design/Completion** 2002/2003 | **Architect** Zhang Wei, Chen Zhuoru

透视图二

Project Shanghai Greentown Yangdong Estate
Location Cross of South Yanggao road and Pujian road, Shanghai
Purpose residential | **Area** 440,000 m² | **Design/Completion** 2002–2004/2007

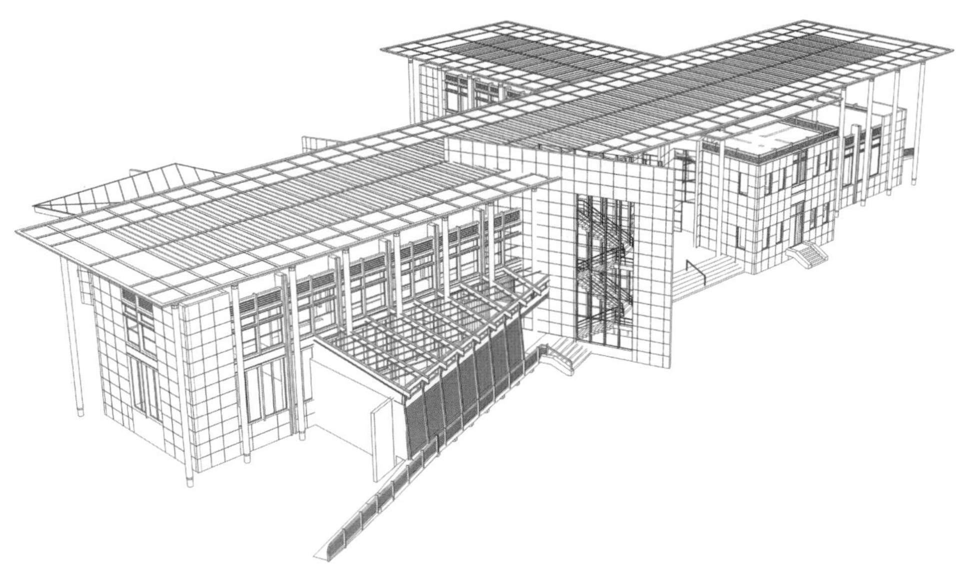

▲
Project Service Center of International Water City
Location Binjiang District, Hangzhou
Purpose offices, exhibition
Area 3,200 m² | **Design/Completion** 2003/2004

Project Office Building of Bank and Assurance Company of Yinzhou County in Ningbo | **Location** Yinzhou District, Ningbo, Zhejiang
Purpose offices | **Area** 50,683 m² | **Design** 2005 | **Architect** Huang Yunian, Wu Weimin, Wu Xuan

TIANHUA ARCHITECTURE PLANNING AND ENGINEERING

▼

Huang Xiangming
Ding Chun
Chen Lei
Nie Xin
Chen Yi

▶ www.thape.com

Founded in 1997 this company is one of the largest private architecture and consulting firms in China. The head office in Shanghai alone employs over 200 people and branches have been opened in Shenzhen and Beijing. Besides the standard offering of architecture and planning services in the field of construction engineering, urban planning, landscape planning and interior design the company also provides services in the areas of consultation, project development and statics and engineering. The company takes its philosophy from the neo-literati architecture school, an offshoot of the Chinese literati architecture represented by the gardens of Suzhou. This new interpretation of traditional forms is also an attempt to sound out a range of possibilities for modern, western-inspired architecture in a far-eastern setting.

Das 1997 gegründete Unternehmen gehört zu den größten privaten Architektur- und Beratungsfirmen Chinas. Allein am Hauptsitz in Shanghai sind mehr als 200 Mitarbeiter beschäftigt; und auch in Shenzhen und Peking wurden Filialen eröffnet. Das Angebotsspektrum umfasst neben den üblichen Architektur- und Planungsleistungen in den Bereichen Hochbau, Stadtplanung, Landschaftsplanung und Innenarchitektur auch Beratung, Projektentwicklung sowie Statik- und Ingenieurleistungen. Die Firmenphilosophie gründet sich auf der sogenannten neo-literati-architecture; eine Weiterentwicklung der chinesischen literati-architecture, wie sie die Gärten von Suzhou repräsentieren. Diese neue Interpretation traditioneller Formen ist auch der Versuch, die verschiedenen Möglichkeiten von moderner, westlich inspirierter Architektur vor einem fernöstlichen Hintergrund auszuloten.

▲ ▶

Project New Space International Business Plaza
Location Kai Xuan road, Changning District
Purpose offices, residential
Area 96,000 m²
Design/Completion 02.2002/08.2005
Architect Huang Xiangming, Huang Zheng

▲
Project Ningshou Building Landscape Design
Location Huang Pu District
Purpose landscape architecture | **Design** 1998
Architect Huang Xiangming

Project Liangcheng District Center
Location South Chezhan road, Shuidian road, Shanghai
Purpose offices, residential, hotel
Area 135,051 m² | **Design** 12.2005
Architect Chen Yi, Jiang Zelei

◀ ▼
Project Zhejiang Quzhou Technical College (phase 2)
Location Jiu Huashan road, Quzhou Zhejiang Province
Purpose education
Area 240,000 m^2
Design/Completion 2003/11.2005
Architect Huang Xiangming, Wu Jihe

▶
Project New Pujiang Town No. 122 Plot
Location Pujiang Town, Minhang District
Purpose residential
Area 248,000 m^2
Design/Completion 2004/2006
Architect Huang Xiangming, Ding Chun, Jiang Zelei

A&S INTERNATIONAL ARCHITECTURAL DESIGN AND CONSULTING

▼

Yu Li
Li Xingguo

▶ www.as-arch.com

Founded in Atlanta, this company has maintained an office in Beijing since 2002. Its architects see it as their job, against the backdrop of China's rush to develop, to bring contemporary international projects from the drawing board stage to completion. The very highest of standards and absolute professionalism go without saying in this architecture office, as does its rejection of fashionable, attention-grabbing projects. In the place of the latter the company favours a highly rational and analytical approach to the search for architectural solutions and a commitment to forging a link between traditional Chinese building styles and modern architecture.

Das Unternehmen, gegründet in Atlanta, hält seit 2002 auch ein Büro in Peking. Ihre Aufgabe sehen die hier arbeitenden Architekten in der Umsetzung internationaler, zeitgenössischer Entwurfs- und Planungsideen vor dem Hintergrund der rasanten Entwicklung in China. Zum Selbstverständnis gehören ein hoher Qualitätsanspruch und absolute Professionalität, aber auch eine gewisse Distanz zu modischen, in erster Linie spektakulären Projekten. Stattdessen setzt man hier auf ein analytisches, streng rationales Vorgehen beim Suchen nach einer architektonischen Lösung und strebt nach einer Verbindung zwischen chinesischen Bautraditionen und moderner Architektur.

▲ ▶ ▼

 Project Chegongzhuang Residential Community (five buildings, Beijing) | **Location** Xicheng District, Beijing

 Purpose commercial, residential | **Area** 168,000 m² | **Design/Completion** 2002/2004 | **Architect** Yu Li

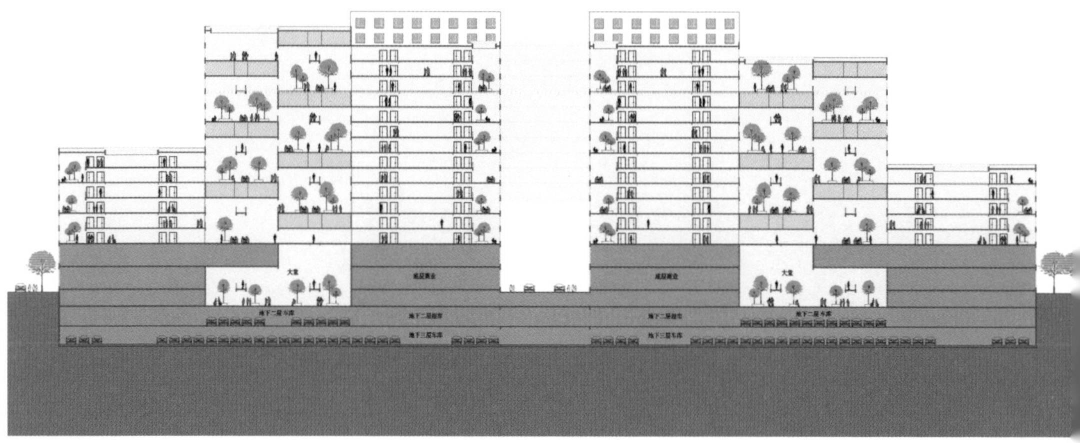
大堂
地下二层车库
地下三层车库
大堂
地下二层车库
地下三层车库

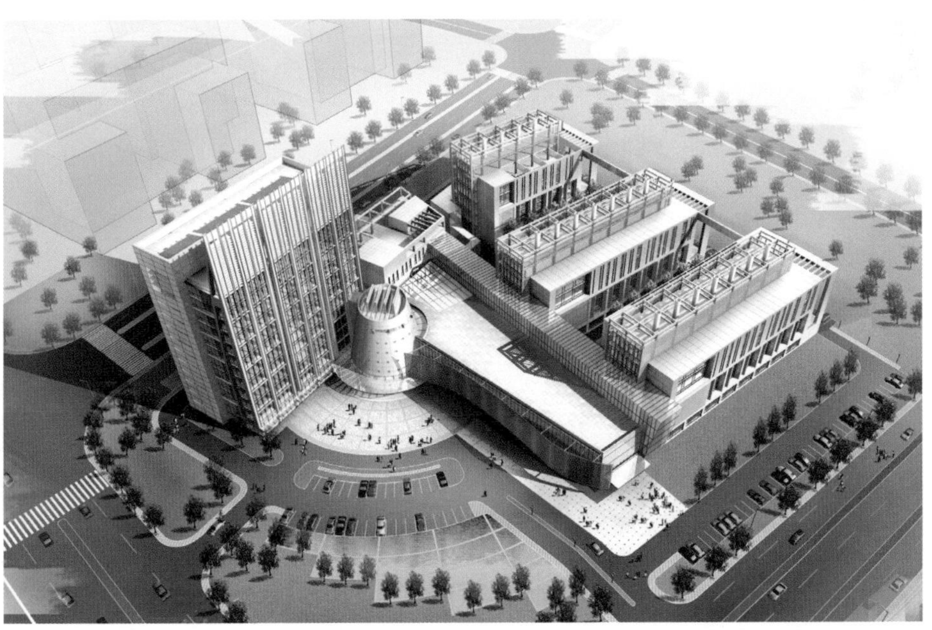

▲

Project Guangzhou CDC (Winner of bidding) | **Location** Guangzhou
Purpose offices | **Area** 120,000 m² | **Design** 2005 | **Architect** Yu Li

Project Beijing Triplex House
Location Beijing
Purpose residential
Area 145,400 m²
Design/Completion 2005/2006
Architect Yu Li

WANG SHIAO SHIONG & ASSOCIATES

▼

Peng Qinfeng

▶ 13803464228@263.net

This company was one of the first architecture firms to receive a licence from the Chinese construction ministry to operate on the private market. Since then it has become an important actor in the construction and real estate sector. The company's clear orientation towards the emerging and growing market has produced an architecture practice that, on the one hand, is heavily geared to the needs of building principals and users and, on the other hand, reflects much of the architects' own professional desire to express themselves. While many of the company's residential projects conform to the current popular trend that is the Europeanisation of Chinese architecture many office blocks and public buildings are obvious references to traditional Chinese building culture. This notwithstanding, the company's large-scale projects are ample proof that the international modern style of architecture has well and truly arrived in China.

Das Büro gehörte zu den ersten Architekturfirmen, die vom Bauministerium Chinas die Lizenz zur Privatisierung erhielten. Seither hat es sich zu einem wichtigen Akteur auf dem Bau- und Immobiliensektor entwickelt. Die klare Ausrichtung am entstehenden und wachsenden Markt hat eine Architektur hervorgebracht, die einerseits stark an den Bedürfnissen der Bauherren und Nutzer orientiert ist, andererseits auch viel vom professionellen Selbstverständnis der Architekten widerspiegelt. Während viele Wohn- und Siedlungsbauten dieses Büros ganz dem populären Trend einer Europäisierung der chinesischen Architektur entsprechen, überraschen nicht wenige Geschäftshäuser und öffentliche Bauten mit klaren Bezügen zur chinesischen Tradition. Dennoch beweisen die Großprojekte dieses Büros, dass die internationale Moderne aus China nicht mehr wegzudenken ist.

▲ ▶

Project Taiyuan Oriental Plaza | **Location** May Day Square, Taiyuan, Shanxi Province
Purpose retail trade, offices | **Area** 567,162 m² | **Design/Completion** 10.2004 | **Architect** Zhao Jinsong, Wu Jie, Cheng Rui

Project Anhui Wuhu Taihua Garden
Location Anhui Province
Purpose residential
Area 21,900 m^2
Design/Completion 1997/1999
Architect Gao Huan, Wu Ben

▲ ▶

Project Taiyuan North America Elegance High-Rise Dwellings
Location Yifen street, Taiyuan
Purpose residential
Area 100,000 m^2
Design/Completion 01.2001/2003
Architect Wang Zhongwen, Wei Hong

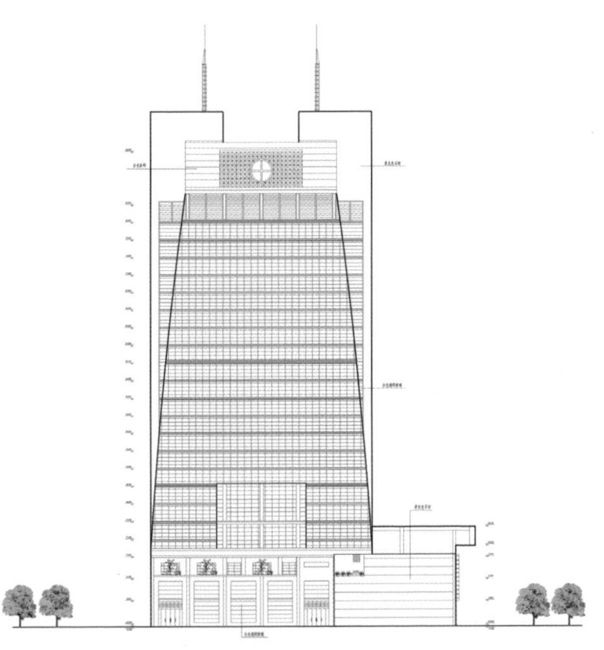

◄

◄

Project Zhuzhou Youth and Children's Palace
Location Zhuzhou, Hunan Province
Purpose leisure
Area 100,000 m²
Architect Peng Qinfeng, Xie Hui

◄ ▼

Project Nanning Logistics Center of Guangxi Post
Location Nanning, Guangxi Province
Purpose offices
Area 34,689 m²
Architect Peng Qinfeng, Xie Hui

TIANJIN ZHONG JIAN ARCHITECTS

Zhang Bo

Hua Jike

▶ www.tjztj.com

This practice employs approx. 70 people. It deliberately rejects the purely commercial architecture of project developers on the one hand and the large, self-indulgent projects of the global avant-garde on the other hand. The company aims to produce »good architecture«, i.e. to produce designs, plans and buildings that take account of people's everyday lives and materialise as a result of dialogue between architects, principals and users. »Good architecture« refers to a form of communication that takes the needs and aspirations of the other side seriously and is responsive to them. Planning is preceded by a detailed study and analysis of framework conditions, the findings of which are made accessible to all parties. This is the only way to anchor architecture firmly within a society.

Das Büro beschäftigt etwa 70 Mitarbeiter und setzt sich mit seinem Ansatz ganz bewusst von der reinen Kommerz-Architektur der Projektentwickler einerseits, aber auch von den selbstverliebten Großprojekten einer globalen Avantgarde andererseits ab. Es geht um »aufrechte Architektur«, also um Entwürfe, Planungen und Bauten, die den Alltag der Menschen berücksichtigen und in einem Dialog zwischen Architekten, Bauherren und Nutzern entstehen. Mit »Aufrichtigkeit« ist eine Form der Kommunikation gemeint, welche die Bedürfnisse und Ansprüche der anderen Seite ernst nimmt und darauf reagiert. Der Planung selbst geht eine genaue Untersuchung und Analyse der Rahmenbedingungen voraus, deren Ergebnisse wiederum auch allen Beteiligten zur Verfügung gestellt werden. Nur auf diese Weise lässt sich Architektur in einer Gesellschaft verankern.

▲ ▶
Project Pingshandao Primary School, Tianjin
Location Qixiangtai road, Hexi District, Tianjin
Purpose education
Area 8,000 m²
Design/Completion 03.2001/01.2004
Architect Lu Yong, Zhang Bo

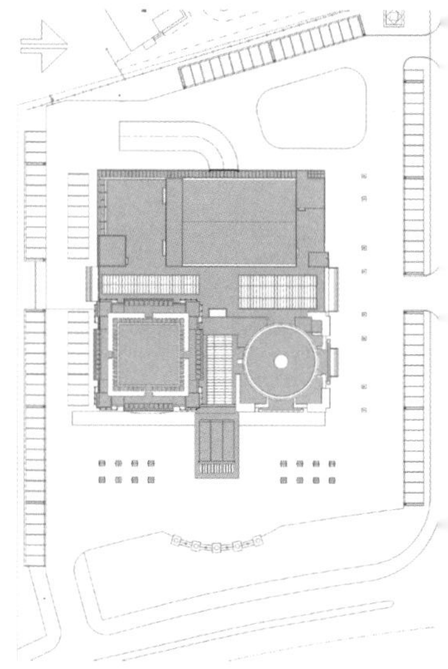

▲ ▶
Project 4# Villa of Architect Corridor in Sunco Suntown
Location Tianjin
Purpose residential
Area 8,000 m²
Design/Completion 03.2003/01.2005
Architect Hua Jike

◀
Project Hitech mansions
Location Huayuan New Technology Industry Area District, Tianjin
Purpose offices
Area 39,000 m²
Design/Completion 07.2001/09.2004
Architect Zhang Bo

Project Tianjin Siyuan Square, Modern Industry Museum and City History Museum
Location Firth of Sancha River, Tianjin
Purpose museum
Area 24,300 m²
Architect MRAC (France), Wang Kening, Zhang Bo

GMB + GMB CHINA

▶ www.gmbarchitects.com

Founded in 2001, this architecture firm has come to be seen as the Chinese branch of the Australia-based GMB Architects and has already notched up a string of small and large projects in China. Besides its comprehensive urban and regional planning at local and district level the company has also built public buildings and an entire rail facility and is involved in consultation and project management. At the planning stage of larger building projects in particular the company's architects place a high value on the human factor, often overlooked. Sustainability is also a key issue for GMB. Designs are drawn up with a view to the ecological consequences for the environment and social and cultural repercussions are also taken into account. By consistently striving to achieve a »green architecture« the planners hope to bind the new Chinese architecture into the international avant-garde school.

Das 2001 gegründete Büro, sozusagen die chinesische Filiale des in Australien sitzenden Unternehmens GMB Architects, kann bereits auf eine Vielzahl realisierter kleinerer und vor allem großer Projekte in China zurückblicken. Neben umfassenden Stadt- und Regionalplanungen sowohl auf kommunaler wie auch auf Bezirksebene gehören dazu öffentliche Bauten sowie eine komplette Eisenbahnanlage. Die Leistungen des Büros umfassen darüber hinaus Beratung und Projektsteuerung. Vor allem bei der Planung größerer Bauten legen die Architekten Wert auf menschliche Dimensionen, die angesichts der schieren Größe der Projekte oft ins Hintertreffen gelangen. Auch das Problem der Nachhaltigkeit spielt eine große Rolle. Ökologische Ansätze gehen in die Entwürfe ebenso ein wie soziale und kulturelle Aspekte. Mit dem konsequenten Streben nach einer »Grünen Architektur« versuchen die Planer, der neuen chinesischen Architektur Anschluss an eine internationale Avantgarde zu verschaffen.

▲▶▼
Project Kunshan Library
Location 353, Middle Qianjin road, Kunshan, Jiangsu Province
Purpose library
Area 18,636 m²
Design/Completion 04.2003/02.2005

Project Suzhou Industrial Park Neighbourhood Center
Location 178, Xinghu street, Suzhou Industrial Park, Jiangsu Province
Purpose leisure | **Area** 28,083 ha
Design/Completion 12.2002/12.2004

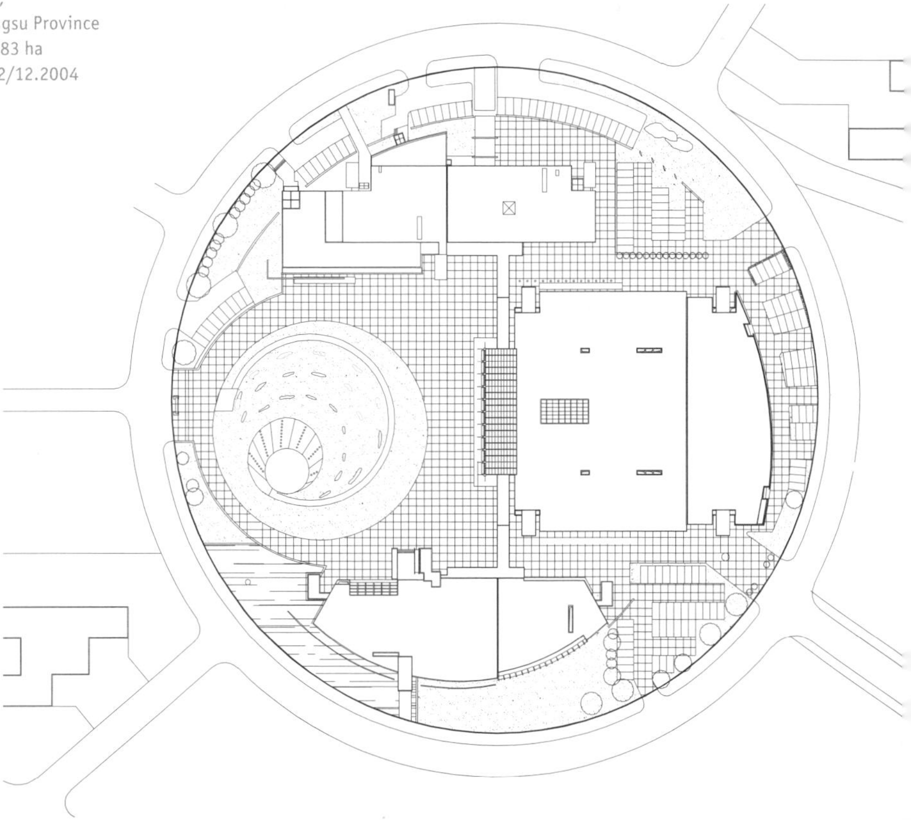

▼
Project Chongqing Art Museum | **Location** Chongqing
Purpose museum | **Design** 2005

▲
Project Suzhou International Education Park – Shared Area Project Design
Location Shangfang Hill at Shihu Lake Resort Area **Purpose** education | **Design** 2004

▶
Project Bei Hang University,
Old and New School District Planning
Location HaiDian District, Beijing
Purpose education
Design 2003

▶
Project Chongqing Science and Technology Museum
Location Chongqing
Purpose museum
Design 2005

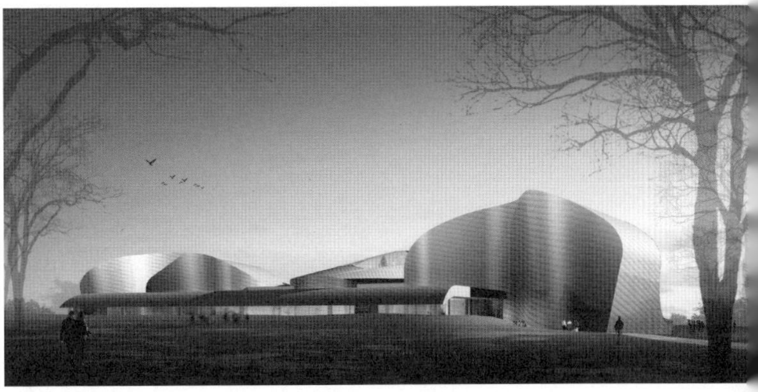

SHZF ARCHITECTURAL DESIGN

▼

Ou Yangkang
Zheng Wenhui
Gong Gefei
Ding Mingyuan
Li Li Lu Zhen
Bao Hailing

▶ www.shzf.com.cn

This institute, created in 1979 and based in Shanghai, has specialised in interior design, landscape planning and master plans for urban development. Since being privatised it has become one of the largest architecture firms in the city. The company is keen to establish its own trademark signature in its building projects and is happy to cite architects gmp (Gerkan, Marg und Partner) from Hamburg in Germany as a model. While many newly formed private architecture firms are still struggling with the last remnants of the myriad state restrictions SHZF has managed to disentangle itself from this condition of dependency. Nonetheless the rampant market in China also contains risks for the development of Chinese architecture, since in a world governed by the dictates of finance it is no easy matter to hold fast to an ideal, as every good architect should be doing.

Das 1979 gegründete Institut mit Sitz in Shanghai hat sich auf städtebauliche Masterpläne, Innenarchitektur und Landschaftsplanung spezialisiert. Seit seiner Privatisierung zählt es zu den größten Architekturfirmen der Stadt. Das Büro strebt nach einer eigenen, unverwechselbaren Handschrift und nennt freimütig die deutschen Architekten gmp (Gerkan, Marg und Partner) aus Hamburg als Vorbild. Während viele der neu gegründeten privaten Architekturbüros noch mit den letzten Überbleibseln der zahllosen staatlichen Restriktionen kämpfen, ist es SHFZ geglückt, sich Schritt für Schritt aus dieser Abhängigkeit zu befreien. Doch auch der ungezügelte Markt in China birgt Risiken für die Entwicklung der Architektur, denn es ist ebenso kompliziert, unter dem mächtigen Diktat des Geldes ein Ideal anzustreben, wie es jeder gute Architekt tun sollte.

▲ ▶

Project San Marino Bridge | **Location** Tangan road, Tang Town, Pudong, Shanghai
Purpose residential | **Area** 39,017 m² | **Design/Completion** 2003/2005 | **Architect** Yu Wei, Chen Jiayuan | **Associate** JWDA

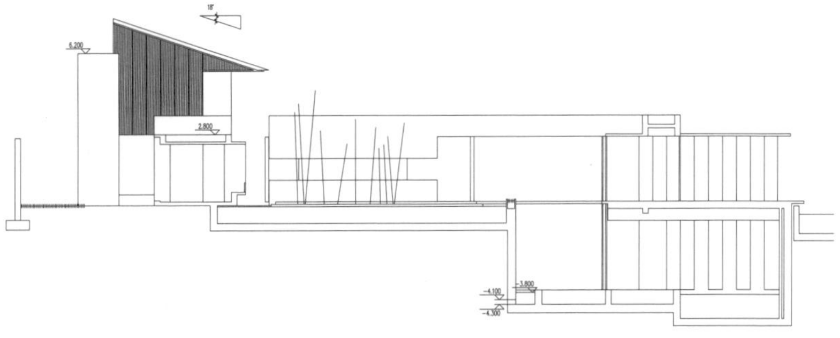

Project Mandarin Palace | **Location** Fangdian road and Jinxiu road, Pudong, Shanghai | **Purpose** residential
Area 28,722 m² | **Design/Completion** 2003/2005 | **Architect** Ding Mingyuan, Lu Zhe

Project Jingding-Anbang Mansion
Location South Wuning road and Kangding road, Jing'an District, Shanghai
Purpose residential
Area 62,258 m²
Design/Completion 2002/2005
Architect Gong Gefei

IMAGEARCHITEKTUR

CHINESISCHE ARCHITEKTUR
AUF DER SUCHE NACH IDENTITÄT UND ZUGEHÖRIGKEIT

HIGH-SPEED-URBANISIERUNG UND HIGH-END-ARCHITEKTUR

Nach langen Jahren am wirtschaftlichen und politischen Rand ist China auf dem Weg, eine neue Supermacht zu werden. Diese Entwicklung ist nicht allein auf das unfassbare Tempo des ökonomischen Wachstums, sondern auch auf das erstarkende kulturelle Selbstbewusstsein des Landes zurückzuführen.

Die in den letzten Jahrzehnten des 20. Jahrhunderts in Gang gekommene Öffnung und Liberalisierung des Landes sowie die nachfolgende Einrichtung von Sonderwirtschaftszonen sorgen für ungebremstes Wachstum in den Kernregionen. Viele Investitionen des Auslands, die Westchina als billigen Produktionsstandort mit guter Infrastruktur oder als größten Absatzmarkt der Welt entdeckt haben, kurbeln den Motor des ökonomischen Fortschritts an. Dass es dem bevölkerungsreichsten Land der Welt gelungen ist, solche globalen Großereignisse wie die Olympischen Spiele 2008 oder die EXPO 2010 für sich zu gewinnen, scheint alle Prognosen zu bestätigen: An China kommt heute niemand mehr vorbei. Die rasante Entwicklung zeitigt vor allem im Land selbst ungeheure Folgen.

China ist in eine Art »Hochgeschwindigkeitsurbanismus«[1] verfallen. Von den 1,3 Milliarden dort lebenden Menschen[2] werden in den nächsten Jahren trotz bereits geltender Zuzugsbeschränkungen etwa 400 bis 500 Millionen in die jetzt schon als Megacities bezeichneten Städte strömen.[3] Sie wollen an dem Wirtschaftsboom teilhaben und treiben die Nachfrage nach Wohnraum und Arbeitsplätzen weiter in die Höhe. Ein Ende dieses Trends ist nicht in Sicht. Er hat gerade erst begonnen.

Shanghai, Beijing und das Pearl-River-Delta sind sicher die bekanntesten Schauplätze einer ungeheuerlich anmutenden Abriss- und Aufbauwelle. Wachstumsprozesse, die in Europa im 19. Jahrhundert vonstattengingen, erfolgen in China zwar mit Verspätung, dafür aber in mehr als doppelter Geschwindigkeit und in wesentlich größeren Maßstäben. Parallel zum Wirtschaftswachstum werden Bauprojekte in beeindruckendem Ausmaß und rasanter Schnelligkeit durchgeführt.

So kann man beobachten, wie in Shanghai fünfzig Stockwerke zählende Hochhäuser binnen kurzer Zeit inmitten traditioneller zweigeschossiger Lilong-Haussiedlungen entstehen und das Viertel völlig verändern. Von den ursprünglich ansässigen Bewohnern bleiben nur die wenigsten.

Zur Entlastung der Metropole Shanghai werden neun vollständig neu geplante Satellitenstädte in extrem kurzer Zeit aus dem Boden gestampft – jede entspricht einem speziellen europäischen Vorbild.[4] Die Stadt Anting

[1] *Titel des Architekturmagazins archplus: Chinesischer Hochgeschwindigkeitsurbanismus, Heft 168, Aachen/Berlin 2004.*

[2] *The World Factbook, Juli 2006.*

[3] *Prof. Wu, Leiter der Architekturfakultät der Tongji Universität Shanghai, in der Süddeutschen Zeitung vom 03.01.2004, Seite 13.*

[4] *Anting, Luodian, Zhujiajiao, Fengcheng, Gaoqiao, Fengjing, Pujiang, Zhoupu, Buzhen (vgl. www.sinocities.net).*

vom deutschen Büro AS&P ähnelt einer deutschen Kleinstadt und ist bereits fertig gestellt – britische, holländische, italienische und spanische Klon-Siedlungen folgen unmittelbar.

Große Abschnitte der Fluss- und Seeufer werden trockengelegt, um den neuen Idealstädten Platz zu machen. Bekannt ist vor allem die Wasserstadt Lingang New City (Luchao Harbour City), entworfen vom deutschen Architekturbüro gmp. Südlich von Shanghai am Chinesischen Meer entsteht auf 74 Quadratkilometern für 800.000 Einwohner eine völlig neue, in konzentrischen Kreisen und Radialachsen organisierte Idealstadt mit einem künstlichen See im Zentrum.[5] Doch dies wird nicht die einzige Siedlung auf dem dem Wasser abgerungenen Land bleiben. Im Golf von Hangzhou soll mit einer Fläche von 250 Quadratkilometern die bisher größte von Grund auf neu geplante Großstadt entstehen. In den Sechzigerjahren noch als zusätzliches Ackerland geplant, wurde für das Areal nun ein Masterplan von SYNIA (Shangyu New Industrial Area) von Fink + Jocher erstellt. Mehr als 800.000 Menschen sollen einmal in diesem Gebiet leben, das eintausendmal größer ist als das Wettbewerbsareal Potsdamer Platz/Leipziger Platz in Berlin.[6]
Noch bis 1978 war Beijing eine etwas über 50 Quadratkilometer große Stadt mit überwiegend ein- bis zweigeschossiger Bebauung. Seit November 2003 umschließen fünf Ringstraßen mit sechs bis zehn, teilweise sogar 14[7] Fahrspuren eine Agglomeration von Hochhäusern auf einer Fläche von etwa 600 Quadratkilometern. Die sechste Ringstraße ist bereits in einer Entfernung von etwa 50 Kilometern vom Stadtkern im Bau. Auch die siebte Ringautobahn wird schon geplant, um dem weiter wachsenden Verkehrsaufkommen und Grundstücksbedarf gerecht werden zu können.

Alte Dörfer, noch vor 20 Jahren weit entfernt von Beijing, sind nun von Hochhaussiedlungen eingekesselt und mutieren zu preiswerten und völlig überfüllten Schlaf- und Dienstleistungsstätten für Heerscharen von Wanderarbeitern. Oder sie werden sukzessive »renoviert«.[8]
Klassische Stadtmodelle reichen schon lange nicht mehr aus, um die Ballung von Siedlungsstrukturen im ostasiatischen Raum zu beschreiben.[9]
China als aufstrebende Wirtschaftsmacht hat ein ungebrochenes Geltungs- und Prestigebedürfnis. Doch auch Firmen, Institutionen und bevorstehende Großereignisse verlangen nach einer neuen markanten und modernen Leuchtturmarchitektur.

Für die Olympischen Spiele 2008 in Beijing entstehen weltweit einzigartige Großprojekte. Beispielhaft für diese ehrgeizige Entwicklung stehen das aufgrund seiner bizarr verschlungenen Konstruktion als »Vogelnest« bezeichnete Stadion der Schweizer Herzog & de Meuron oder auch das Schwimmstadion von PTW Architects aus Australien mit Tragwerk und Kleid aus luftig blauem Schaum.

[5] *Vgl.: www.gmp-architekten.de*

[6] *Vgl.: www.fink-jocher.de*

[7] *Zweimal vier Fahrspuren auf der Hauptstraße und zusätzlich zweimal drei parallel geführte Fahrspuren für Nahverkehr und Abbieger.*

[8] *Renovieren heißt in diesem Fall: Komplettabriss und Neubau von Wohnhochhäusern oder Grünanlagen. Vgl. Barbara Münch, Michael Arri: Simultane Realitäten – Urban Villages in Chinas expandierenden Metropolen, in: Gregor Jansen: totalstadt.beijing case. High Speed Urbanisierung in China, Köln 2006, S. 188-195.*

[9] *Neue Begriffe müssen erfunden werden, um diese Phänomene zu beschreiben. Siehe hier insbesondere Chuihua J. Chung, Jeffrey Inhaba, Rem Koolhaas: Great Leap Forward: Harvard Design School Project on the City, Köln 2001; Peter G. Rowe: East Asia Modern: Shaping the Contemporary City, London 2005.*

Im neuen Central Business District von Beijing wird neben etwa 300 neuen Hochhäusern die Zentrale des chinesischen Fernsehens CCTV nach dem Entwurf von Rem Koolhaas und Ole Scheeren errichtet. Mit seiner besonders auffälligen Form gilt dieses Bauwerk schon jetzt als Markenzeichen des Senders, der auch die Übertragung der Olympischen Spiele organisieren wird. Kein Wunder, dass die Baustelle des über 230 Meter in den Himmel ragenden »Loop« mehr Aufmerksamkeit bekommt als jede andere.[10]
In Shanghai führt die EXPO 2010 zu ähnlichen Auswüchsen architektonischer Selbstinszenierung. Neben der Darstellung der Wirtschaftskraft im neuen »Financial and Business District« und dem Ausdruck technologischer Stärke im »Shanghai Science & Technology Museum«[11] hat die Stadt den Ehrgeiz, auch ihre kulturelle Vorreiterrolle zu demonstrieren. Während in vielen europäischen Großstädten Konzertsäle und Opernhäuser schließen müssen, weil sich die Kommunen nur eine Kulturstätte leisten können, eröffnet in Shanghai zusätzlich zur 1998 fertig gestellten Oper des Architekten Jean Marie Charpentier, dem 2004 sanierten und um 60 Meter verschobenen Konzerthaus und einem Dutzend weiterer Spielstätten der nächste große, 3.300 Zuschauer fassende Entertainmentkomplex des französischen Architekten Paul Andreu.[12]

Beijing, Shanghai, Shenzhen sowie auch Guangzhou und Chongqing planen Wolkenkratzer mit Rekordmaßen.[13] Der 610 Meter hohe Fernseh- und Sightseeingtower in Guangzhou von Arup/Information Based Architecture wird voraussichtlich schon 2009 fertig gestellt.
Shanghai und Beijing wollen als »Global City« wahrgenommen werden und sich mit Metropolen wie New York oder London messen können. Innerhalb des Landes ringen Provinzhauptstädte mit ähnlichen Mitteln um Aufmerksamkeit im Machtverteilungskampf. Sie schmücken sich mit völlig überdimensionierten Hochhäusern, Kongresscentern, Konzerthäusern und Ausstellungshallen, um wenigstens mit einem neuen, am Reißbrett entworfenen Wahrzeichen einen gewissen Hauch von Größe vermitteln zu können.

China ist wohl das einzige Land, in dem sich Projekte in extrem kurzer Zeit und ungeheuren Dimensionen realisieren lassen.[14] Selbst kleinere Büros, wie beispielsweise Fink + Jocher aus München, haben in China die Chance, große Projekte zu bearbeiten, freilich nur, wenn sie sich auf chinesische Gegebenheiten einlassen und nach mitunter Nerven zehrenden Wartezeiten rasch und umstandslos zur Stelle sind.
Die chinesischen Investoren vertrauen sehr auf westliches Know-how. Allerdings dürfen ausländische Büros in der Regel ausschließlich als »Design«-Büros auftreten. Eine Zusammenarbeit mit einem großen lizenzierten chinesischen Planungsinstitut ist quasi Pflicht. Diese erzwungene Arbeitsteilung hat ihren Grund in der zweigeteilten Struktur des chinesischen Planungswesens – auch chinesische Designbüros entwerfen oft nur bunte Perspektiven von Gebäuden. Die Ausführung müssen sie einem der Institute

[10] Vgl. Sebastian Redecke: OMA, Arup und das CCTV, Bauwelt 07/2007, S. 14.
[11] Entworfen von RTKL Associates, 2001.
[12] Feierlich eröffnet am 31. Dezember 2004.
[13] 2007 ist der höchste Wolkenkratzer das »Taipei Financial Center – Taipei 101« in Taiwan mit 508 Metern Höhe.
[14] Vgl. Deyan Sudjic: Die Karawane zieht weiter, in: archplus, Heft 168, Aachen/Berlin 2004, S. 30-32.
[15] Vgl. Eduard Kögel: Zur Lage junger Architekten in China, in: archplus, Heft 168, Aachen/Berlin 2004, S. 71f.

überlassen, die auf Kosten sparendes und standardisiertes Bauen spezialisiert sind.[15] So entsprechen die Ausführungen oft nicht den Vorstellungen der Architekturbüros, weil speziell entwickelte Lösungen von den Planungsinstituten durch Standarddetails ersetzt werden. Manchmal werden dann aus ursprünglich filigranen Stahlkonstruktionen auf diese Weise schwerfällige Stahlbetonklötze. Zur Sicherung der Qualität bleibt häufig nur die Möglichkeit, international arbeitende Ingenieurbetriebe und Ausführungsfirmen in das Projekt zu integrieren.

IDENTITÄTSPROBLEME

Die Architektur internationaler Büros ist zunehmend chinesischer Kritik ausgesetzt. So sei zum Beispiel die Oper von Paul Andreu zu unchinesisch, nicht dem Kontext der Umgebung angepasst. Außerdem wäre zu viel des knappen Rohstoffs Stahl verbaut worden, was das Projekt unnötig verteuerte. Ähnliche Kritik müssen sich auch Rem Koolhaas für seinen CCTV-Tower und Herzog & de Meuron für ihr Olympiastadion anhören. In den chinesischen Medien werden Stimmen laut, die den ausländischen Architekten vorwerfen, die Kultur Chinas nicht zu verstehen und sich arrogant über Chinas Bedürfnisse hinwegzusetzen. Die Kritiken gipfeln in dem Verdacht, ausländische Architekten benutzten China als Spielfeld für ihre experimentellen Ideen.[16] Es wurde sogar diskutiert, ob ausländische Büros bei bestimmten Projekten und Wettbewerben ausgeschlossen werden sollten.

Doch trotzdem bekommen die chinesischen Designinstitute seltener Aufträge für nationale Prestigeprojekte als ihre Kollegen aus dem Ausland. Den bekannten Namen des internationalen Architekten braucht man für solche Vorhaben ebenso wie dessen Erfahrung mit Großprojekten. Nicht umsonst werden gerade jene Architekten ausgewählt, die auch Preisträger des wichtigsten internationalen Architekturpreises – des Pritzker-Prize – sind oder auf ähnlich reputierliche Ehrungen verweisen können.

China hat ein Identitätsproblem. Das belegen mehr als deutlich die von den ausländischen Architekturbüros errichteten holländischen Siedlungen mit Windmühlen, die englischen Städte im Tudor-Stil und die italienischen Quartiere mit Piazza und Canale. Doch sind es chinesische Investoren und Führungskräfte, die auf Marktplätzen nach deutschem Vorbild Schiller und Goethe platziert haben möchten.
Dass nach der lange ungebrochenen Glorifizierung ausländischer Architektur die Kritik plötzlich mit dem Kampfbegriff Identität und der nicht verstandenen chinesischen Kultur ansetzt, ist daher nicht verwunderlich. Diese Diskussion ist weltweit eng mit globalen Prozessen verknüpft. Sie setzt dann ein, wenn eine zunehmende Globalisierung als Angriff auf gesellschaftliche und kulturelle Werte und Traditionen verstanden wird. Denn die ökonomische und kulturelle Globalisierung erzeugt eine Homogenisierung,

[16] *Vgl. Zhang Hong: Beijing: Architectural Showcase, in: China today, vol. 02/2005.*

die nationale Unterschiede und regionale Eigenheiten verschwinden lässt. Dies hat besonders im neuen »Global Player« China Auswirkungen auf die Architektur.

Doch worin besteht die Identität der chinesischen Gesellschaft? Was sind ihre Merkmale, womit kann sie sich identifizieren, und wie unterscheidet sie sich von anderen? Von außen durch die Medien oder als Tourist betrachtet, erscheint China als eine große einheitliche Nation. Auch die Chinesen selbst sind davon überzeugt. Das hat verschiedene Ursachen: Im Bewusstsein der Chinesen ist ihre Kultur die älteste der Welt. Schon 1000 v. Chr. nachweisbar, reicht sie angeblich noch viel weiter, bis in mythische Zeiten zurück: Bereits 2205 v. Chr. soll der legendäre Kaiser Yu die Xia-Dynastie gegründet und damit den Grundstein für eine über 4.000 Jahre andauernde Hochkultur gelegt haben. Erstaunlich dabei ist die Kontinuität, die die chinesische Kulturentwicklung aufweist. Tatsächlich kann kein anderes Volk der Welt über einen so langen Zeitraum hinweg als einheitlicher und klar abgegrenzter Kulturraum betrachtet werden. Es gibt ein starkes Bewusstsein dafür, dass China schon immer eine große Kultur gewesen ist. Die Stärke der langen gemeinsamen Geschichte hält das chinesische Volk auch in der Gegenwart und Zukunft zusammen.

Zweite Ursache ist die chinesische Sonderform des »frühkapitalistischen Kommunismus«, die als autoritäres System in der Lage ist, eine Nation von 1,3 Milliarden Menschen zusammenzuhalten und zu kontrollieren.

Die dritte Ursache ist das derzeitige Wirtschaftswachstum. Eine positive Grundstimmung, die auf nationaler Ebene erzeugt wird, wirkt auch ansteckend auf westliche Nationen, die an dieser Entwicklung teilhaben wollen. Chinas größter Wunsch ist es, als moderner Staat mit langer Tradition wahrgenommen zu werden. Doch die suggerierte nationale Homogenität gibt es nicht. China ist nicht die einheitliche Nation, die sich nun in klarer Fortsetzung eigener Traditionen komplett modernisiert. Die Brüche sind unübersehbar.

Deutlichster Gegensatz ist dabei der Konflikt zwischen Tradition und Moderne. Durch die lange Geschichte besteht eine große Verbundenheit zur eigenen Kulturgeschichte. Viele Elemente des alten China, des Buddhismus, des Taoismus und des Konfuzianismus spielen auch heute noch eine wichtige Rolle in der Gesellschaft. Sie gelten nicht nur als Maßstäbe für das eigentlich Chinesische, sondern dienen auch der Abgrenzung gegenüber kulturellen Importen aus anderen Teilen der Welt. Daraus resultiert zwangsläufig eine auf die Vergangenheit bezogene Sichtweise. Auf der anderen Seite erzeugen der Wirtschaftsboom und die auf globale Mechanismen reagierende Nation den Wunsch nach einem neuen China, das losgelöst von alten hinderlichen Traditionen ist. Dieses Nebeneinander von Traditionsbewusstsein und dem Streben nach Zugehörigkeit zur globalen, post-industriellen Gesellschaft muss zu Verwerfungen führen.

Während die ältere Bevölkerung stärker mit den traditionellen Lebensweisen verbunden ist, distanziert sich die Jugend zunehmend vom überlieferten

Werte- und Normensystem. Vor 20 Jahren wurden Alltagsprobleme in Familien- oder Arbeitsgemeinschaften (sogenannten Danweis) gelöst. Sie können als Fortsetzung des konfuzianischen gesellschaftlichen Ordnungssystems interpretiert werden.[17] Nun wächst eine verwöhnte Generation von Einzelkindern heran, die geprägt ist von einer westlich geprägten Vergötterung der Individualität sowie von Konsum und MTV-Kultur. Viele Jugendliche haben ein völlig neues Selbstbewusstsein entwickelt. Sie träumen von einem Aufenthalt im Ausland und einem interessanten Beruf, in dem sie sich verwirklichen können. Eine Elterngeneration, die auf die Einhaltung traditioneller Gemeinschaftsprinzipien besteht, trifft auf eine fremde Jugend mit ganz anderen, eigenen Ansichten und Lebenszielen.

Zu diesem Generationskonflikt gesellt sich das Gefälle zwischen Stadt und Land. Shanghai, Beijing und das Pearl-River-Delta sind Motoren des überall auf der Welt wahrgenommenen »Hochgeschwindigkeits- Urbanismus«. Doch diese Wachstumsphänomene betreffen nur die Städte an der Ostküste und Beijing. Kleine Städte wie Suzhou und Shenzhen, die sich in der Nähe der Metropolen befinden, schwimmen noch im Fahrwasser der Megacities. Ob diese Entwicklung ganz China erreichen wird, ist sehr fraglich. In den Regionen außerhalb des Einflussbereichs der Sonderwirtschaftszonen sieht es ganz anders aus. Weit entfernte Städte wie Chongqing – mit 32 Millionen Einwohnern die größte Stadt der Welt – haben ein wesentlich langsameres Wachstum. Lediglich einige Großprojekte von gesamtstaatlicher Bedeutung – Staudämme oder Kraftwerke – werden auf ganz China verteilt. Die ländlichen Regionen scheinen in ihrer Entwicklung zurückgelassen worden zu sein. Fast feudale Strukturen, Rückständigkeit und große Armut prägen hier das Bild.

Bis vor Kurzem noch hatte das Steuersystem jeden Chinesen verpflichtet, einen hohen finanziellen Beitrag zur Modernisierung der Sonderwirtschaftszonen zu leisten. Ländliche Entwicklung wurde damit ausgebremst. Große Teile der Landbevölkerung wurden an den Rand ihrer Existenz gebracht – eine der Hauptursachen der Landflucht und der starken Bewegung der Wanderarbeiter, die in die Städte strömen. Nun sollen Infrastruktur-Förderprogramme mit Namen wie »Aufbau sozialistischer Dörfer neuen Typs«[18] den kleinen Städten die Möglichkeit geben, ein wenig vom wirtschaftlichen Aufschwung zu profitieren. Doch die Entwicklung schreitet nur langsam voran. Die Politik kann die Folgen der einseitigen Förderung der Sonderwirtschaftszonen und der Vernachlässigung des Hinterlandes nicht auf einen Schlag beseitigen. Angesichts dieser Gegensätze kann von einer einheitlichen chinesischen Identität nicht die Rede sein.

WESTLICHE ARCHITEKTUR WIRD ZUR CHINESISCHEN MODERNE

Die rasch hochgezogenen Gebäude in einem »Business District« sollen vor allem Modernität vermitteln. Es geht um Außenwirkung und Image. Deshalb sind Stil und Symbole die wesentlichen Entwurfskriterien eines Hauses.

[17] Barbara Münch: Verborgene Kontinuitäten des chinesischen Urbanismus, in: archplus, Heft 168, Aachen/Berlin 2004, S.44-49.

[18] Lan Xinzhen: Aufbau sozialistischer Dörfer neuen Typs, in: Beijing Rundschau, 15/2006.

Die chinesische Architektur ist allerdings damit überfordert, passende Bilder mit einer eigenen Identität in hohem Tempo zu produzieren. Daher wird weniger an spezifischen Konzepten gearbeitet als vielmehr auf standardisierte Muster aus westlichen Ländern zurückgegriffen, die in China als modern gelten. Westliche Architekturzeitschriften werden als Mustervorlage für Entwürfe benutzt wie die Baubücher des 19. Jahrhunderts.[19]
Oft muss das Haus bereits verkauft sein, bevor es fertig gestellt ist. So sind nicht Ausführungspläne und Leitdetails die wichtigsten entscheidenden Ergebnisse eines Planungsprozesses, sondern die Renderings eines Hauses – nach den jeweiligen Verkaufsargumenten versehen mit Wasserflächen, Springbrunnen, Lichteffekten, Vögeln oder Flugzeugen. Dazu gehören passende, aus anglo- oder europhonen Versatzstücken zusammengebastelte Fantasienamen wie »Wonderland«, »Dance Moma«, »Soho«, »Western Paradise« oder auch »Rheinstein«.[20]
Die Architektur, die dabei entsteht, verschwindet hinter ihrem bedeutungsüberladenen Image. Viele ringen mit ähnlichen Mitteln um Aufmerksamkeit. Es entstehen auffällige Gebäude, die alle nach einem ähnlichen Schnittmuster gefertigt sind. Nicht Abwechslung und Individualität sind das Ziel, sondern eine bestimmte Außenwirkung, die Zugehörigkeit signalisieren soll: entweder zur modernen Welt oder zur Nation China.
Zu den Gebäuden, die die neue Wirtschaftskraft vermitteln sollen, gehören insbesondere sogenannte »Exhibitionhalls«. Diese Bauten werden oft als Stahl-Glas-Konstruktionen errichtet, die ein alles überspannendes, dynamisches Flugdach als markantes Erkennungszeichen besitzen. Da sich die Bauwerke alle sehr ähnlich sind, geht das Ziel der Hervorhebung gegenüber den anderen verloren. Oft sind die Hallen wenig genutzt, entweder aufgrund ihrer Lage weit außerhalb in einem neu errichteten »New District« oder »Business District« oder wegen ihrer unzulänglichen Grundrisskonfigurationen. Dies ist nicht problematisch, da der Hauptzweck dieser Bauten in der Repräsentation liegt und nicht in einer flexiblen oder intensiven Nutzung. Abbildungen der Fassade schmücken lokale Veranstaltungsblätter und Infobroschüren für Investoren. Außerdem werden gern Schulklassen und Hochzeitspaare vor solchen Gebäuden fotografiert. Das Konzept funktioniert gut. Eine zeichenhafte Identifikation der Bevölkerung mit den Symbolen der Moderne findet statt, solange der Wunsch nach Distanzierung von der Tradition besteht.

Es muss aber nicht immer die Moderne sein. Tempo, Beliebigkeit und Fantasielosigkeit führen zu allen möglichen Ausprägungen einer fast eins zu eins kopierten Architektur Europas.
Besonders im Wohnungsbau werden durch klassische Formen oder auch Stile europäischer Urlaubsregionen heimelige Atmosphären erzeugt. So entstehen Wohnsiedlungen, die an Themenparks erinnern. Schmetterlingsformen oder Musikinstrumente, spanische Dörfer oder griechische Tempelanlagen lassen nicht mehr erkennen, dass viele alte Hofhausbewohner

[19] In China war Architektur bis ins 19. Jahrhundert ein reines Handwerk. Gebaut wurde nach Baubüchern, die exakt vorgaben, wie welche Bauaufgaben ausgeführt werden müssen. Bekanntestes Beispiel sind die sehr lange gültigen »Yingzao Fashi« (Baunormen) von Li Jie, aus dem Jahr 1103 n. Chr. Vgl. Guo Qinghua: Yingzao Fashi: Twelfth-Century Chinese Building Manual, in: Architectural History: Journal of the Society of Architectural Historians of Great Britain, 41/1998.

[20] Shenzhen Wonderland Phase IV – Vanke Developer; Dance Moma – Steiner Modern Engineering & Project Management Co., Ltd.; Western Paradise Walk – Loghu Real Estate; Rheinstein – Beijing Rheinstein Equestrian Center Ltd.; Jianwai SOHO – SOHO China Ltd.

hierfür vorher enteignet wurden. Die neuen Wohnungen werden je nach Geschmack in passenden Stilen wie »Imperial Ecclectic Style«, »European Modern Style« oder »Beyond Vision Style« eingerichtet. Mit blinkenden Plastikpalmen im Innenhof und einem klangvollen Namen der Siedlung haben sich die Wünsche und Träume in Architektur erfüllt. Ein temporärer Verkaufspavillon, der alle Sinne überreizt, komplettiert das Bild.

DIE ROLLE DER TRADITIONELLEN CHINESISCHEN ARCHITEKTUR

Bei Gebäuden, bei denen das spezifisch Chinesische eine wesentliche Rolle spielt, wird oft die eigene Baugeschichte zur Erzeugung von Images herangezogen. Schließlich kann China auf eine über 3.000-jährige Geschichte zurückblicken. Doch zeitigen die Versuche der Bezugnahme allzu oft sehr zwiespältige Ergebnisse.

Die kreisrunde Öffnung als Eingang in den Hof des traditionellen chinesischen Hofhauses ist in der konfuzianischen und taoistischen Lehre verankert. Die Übernahme solcher Stilmittel in den heutigen Hochhausbau ist jedoch meist von deren ursprünglichen Bedeutung losgelöst. Auch die Ära der wahllos und flächendeckend auf alle Gebäude aufgesetzten, in traditioneller Art geschwungenen Dächer auf Neubauten dauert immer noch an.

Diese oberflächliche Übernahme überlieferter Stilmittel lässt bei den Menschen in China die Überzeugung wachsen, dass ein Gebäude chinesisch ist und ihrer Kultur entspricht. Architektur mit schwebenden Metalldächern und Stahl-Glas-Fassaden wird als fremd empfunden – auch wenn sie inzwischen den größten Teil der Bautätigkeit in China ausmacht. Dass diese Form der Architektur importiert wurde, ist den Menschen bewusst.

Gleichwohl ist es erstaunlich, dass die Symbole des alten China immer noch verstanden werden. Chinesische Zitate wie bestimmte Farben, Formen und Zeichen werden erkannt und richtig gedeutet. Lediglich die dabei zu beachtenden Regeln und Verbote werden vernachlässigt. So durften im alten China ausschließlich die kaiserlichen Gebäude gelbe Dächer besitzen. Heute gibt es viele Häuser in Beijing, die gelbe Dächer zitieren, weil diese für Glück, Macht und Weisheit stehen. Dies zeigt deutlich, dass der Inhalt der Zeichen zwar eine Rolle spielt, die Bedeutung aber allmählich verloren geht. Bestimmte Traditionen jedoch erweisen sich als sehr stark, vor allem, wenn es um verheißungsvolle Symbole geht. So gilt Weiß nach wie vor als Trauerfarbe; dreieckige Strukturen oder Gliederungen in sieben Elemente sind nicht beliebt.

Insbesondere in Gebieten mit touristischem Schwerpunkt werden aus Imagegründen komplette Straßenzüge, Viertel oder sogar ganze Städte in traditioneller Bauweise wiedererrichtet. Parks werden mit klassischer Pavillonarchitektur ergänzt und Pagoden, Tempel und Paläste neu aufgebaut.

Da Shanghai keine Altstadt mehr hat, wird um das einzig historisch erhaltene Teehaus eine neue »Altstadt« errichtet. Die Stadtmauer von Xi'an ist nicht vollständig erhalten. Ein Neubau ersetzt nun die fehlenden Teile. Auch in Kaifeng, der Hauptstadt der Song-Dynastie, ist es wichtig, ein besonders traditionelles chinesisches Image zu transportieren. Hierzu wurde schon früh begonnen, eine neue Einkaufsstraße im historischen Stil aufzubauen, die zum alten Drachentempel hinaufführt. Für die anschließende Erweiterung müssen jedoch noch erhaltene Hofhaussiedlungen abgerissen werden.

Auch im Altstadtviertel Beijings werden alte Hofhaussiedlungen gegen den Protest[21] der enteigneten Bewohner abgerissen und durch neue Luxushofhäuser ersetzt. Das Hofhaus wird auf ein Gestaltungsprinzip reduziert,die Vermarktung des Grundstücks optimiert. Was bleibt, sind graue Wände und rote Bemalung. Die ursprüngliche Bevölkerung wird in Neubauviertel weit außerhalb von Beijing gedrängt oder unangemessen entschädigt.[22]

Man bekommt den Eindruck, dass die Chinesen eine neue Liebe zu ihrer eigenen historischen Architektur entwickelt haben, die sie nun auf ähnliche Weise fasziniert wie westliche Touristen – sie ist exotisch. Dem übererfüllten Wunsch nach Modernisierung folgt der verklärte Blick in die Vergangenheit. Doch die unreflektierten Kopien behindern eine Weiterentwicklung der eigenen Traditionen massiv.
Das Stadtviertel Xingtiandi in Shanghai, umgestaltet von den amerikanischen Architekten Benjamin Wood & Carlos Zapata, ist das erste Projekt, in dem ein altes Stadtviertel mit traditionellen Lilong-Häusern revitalisiert wurde. Im Vergleich zu den anderen Vorhaben ist dies ein gewaltiger Fortschritt. Allerdings wurde auch hier der ursprüngliche Charakter, das im Lilong einzigartige soziale Netzwerk, nicht konserviert. Als erhaltenswert erwiesen sich lediglich Teile der baulichen Struktur und Fassaden. Heute ist das Viertel mit seinen internationalen Caféhausketten, Designerbars und Edelrestaurants eines der angesagten Ausgehquartiere der Metropole. Aufgrund des Erfolgs hat diese Form des Umgangs mit alten Stadtstrukturen schon einige Nachahmer gefunden. So wurde beispielsweise auch das Gebiet »Bridge 8« in unmittelbarer Nähe zum Kreativ-Gewerbeareal mit Büros, Shops und Showrooms umgebaut.

Als erhaltenswert und verwertbar gilt fast ausschließlich Architektur, die vor 1911 errichtet wurde. Man hat den Eindruck, im Bewusstsein der Chinesen ist das ursprünglich Chinesische mit der Revolution beendet worden. Der sehnliche Wunsch nach Kontinuität blendet die schmerzhaften Brüche der letzten Jahrzehnte einfach aus.

Allerdings lässt sich seit einer Weile beobachten, dass alte Industrieanlagen zu Galerie- und Künstlerhöfen umgebaut werden. Das Künstlerviertel »Maschinenfabrik 798« nimmt hierbei eine Vorreiterrolle ein. Die freie Künstlerszene Beijings besetzte erfolgreich die 1956 von DDR-Ingenieuren erbauten Industriehallen und nutzt den Industrie-Chic für die Inszenierungen

[21] Proteste sind fast immer vergebens. Auch bekannte Künstler, wie Ai Wei Wei oder Zhang Dali machen auf die Probleme regelmäßig aufmerksam. Bisher ist nur ein Fall eines Kongfu-Meisters aus Chongqing bekannt, der es schaffte, eine bessere Entschädigung zu erzwingen. Vgl. Kirstin Wenk: »Ein Paar kämpft um sein Haus – und wird berühmt, in: Die Welt, 25. 03. 2007; Diess.: Entschädigung für Protestpaar: Haus in Chongqing abgerissen, in: Die Welt, 03.04.2007; vgl. auch Beiträge von Zhang Jie, Wang Jun und Ou Ning in: Gregor Jansen: totalstadt.beijing case. High Speed Urbanisierung in China, Köln 2006.

[22] Vgl. Philippe Pataud Célérier: Spekulation in Shanghai, in: Le Monde Diplomatique 1/2007.

alternativer Projekte. Kommerzielle Konzepte folgen dem Fabrikästhetiktrend – im nördlichen Stadtzentrum von Shanghai wurde mit »The New Factories« eine 1928 errichtete Industrieanlage zur Event- und Freizeitmeile umgebaut. Ähnliche Vorhaben werden auch in Chongqing und Hangzhou realisiert. Ein wesentlich sensiblerer Umgang mit Altbausubstanz unabhängig von spezifischen Stilrichtungen zeichnet sich ab.

ÖKOLOGIE ALS IMAGE

Unabhängig von größeren Trends entwickelt sich auch eine neue Form energiesparender und ökologischer Architektur in China. Noch sind vor allem nur deren Ziele hoch, während es an der Umsetzung bisher hapert. Sie wird aber mit Hilfe staatlicher Förderung von höchster Ebene zunehmend Verbreitung finden und der Architektur in China ein neues Betätigungsfeld eröffnen.

Der ökologische Aspekt ist aus der europäischen Architektur nicht mehr wegzudenken, strenge Umweltauflagen haben inzwischen in allen europäischen Baugesetzen Einzug gehalten. Dies wird auch im Reich der Mitte wahrgenommen – ökologische Architektur dient als Modernitätsindikator. Umweltfreundliche Technologien werden verwendet, um der Welt ein zeitgemäßeres Image präsentieren zu können. Ganz deutlich ist dies an den Vorhaben zur EXPO 2010 zu sehen.

Zu deren Vorbereitung wurde eine Kooperationsinitiative zwischen Hamburg und Shanghai gegründet, um energiesparendes und ökologisches Bauen zu fördern. Die Ecobuild 2006 stellte neun Bauprojekte vor, die den Energieverbrauch gegenüber herkömmlichen Gebäuden um 75 Prozent verringern. Projekte wie das Pujiang Intelligence Valley, ein hocheffizientes Bürogebäude mit 12.000 Quadratmetern Nutzfläche, sind viel besuchte Vorzeigeobjekte, die Nachahmer finden werden.[23]

Das größte Projekt im Rahmen der EXPO 2010 in Shanghai, die unter Motto »Better City, Better Life« steht, ist die neue Satellitenstadt Dongtan Eco City. Hier werden Ökologiekonzepte miteinander kombiniert – nicht unbedingt neu, dafür allerdings äußerst konsequent. Begrenzte Bauhöhen, begrünte Dächer und verkehrsfreie Zonen prägen das Bild. Versorgt wird die Stadt ausschließlich aus erneuerbaren Energien (Windkraft, Photovoltaik, Biomasse). Eigene Wasserwiederaufbereitung und Abfallrecycling ergänzen das Konzept. Die Stadt soll die Umweltstandards der westlichen Welt weit übertreffen.

Auch die Olympischen Spiele in Beijing haben ähnliche Kriterien in ihren fortschrittlichen Zielen verankert: »Grüne Spiele« sollen es werden.[24] So hat man sich zum Beispiel das Ziel gesetzt, mindestens 230 Tage im Jahr den Himmel »blau« erscheinen zu lassen, wozu die Schadstoffbelastung erheblich verringert werden soll. Die Stadt muss wenigstens in den drei entscheidenden Wochen, wenn Gäste aus aller Welt zu Besuch sind, ein

[23] *Vgl. www.green-shanghai.com, www.mudi.com*
[24] *Vgl. http://en.beijing2008.cn*

umweltfreundliches Image besitzen. Dies wird in chinesischer Manier und üblichem Maßstab mit allen Mitteln durchgeführt. Es werden Großbetriebe verlegt oder geschlossen und fünf neue U-Bahnlinien gebaut,[25] über 800 Hektar Grünflächen in der Innenstadt Beijings angelegt,[26] Aufforstungsprogramme für über 10.700 Hektar Wald umgesetzt[27] und in entscheidenden Momenten umfassende Fahrverbote erteilt. Auch die Dächer werden in großem Maßstab begrünt, um schon von oben, insbesondere in der Einflugschneise des Flughafens, einen umweltfreundlicheren Eindruck zu vermitteln. Ökologische Strategien werden nicht aufgrund eines ökologischen Bewusstseins ergriffen, sondern aufgrund eines hypermodernen und westlichen Images, das sie verkörpern.

Ein zweiter Aspekt zum Thema Ökologie gewinnt aber zunehmend an Bedeutung, da er wirtschaftliche Interessen berührt. Das ungebremste Wirtschaftswachstum ist bedroht, da Energieressourcen knapp und Standortnachteile durch Umweltverschmutzung spürbar werden. Die Umweltbelastung wächst mit der Wirtschaft. Umweltverschmutzung ist inzwischen ein Problem mit nationalen Ausmaßen. Laut der IEA-Studie ist China gemessen an der Menge der CO_2-Erzeugung bereits Umweltsünder Nummer zwei weltweit und wird die USA im Jahr 2010 überholen.[28]
Der Einsatz energiesparender Technologien ist notwendig, um im gleichen Tempo weiterwachsen zu können. Der 11. Fünfjahresplan (2006-2010) setzt einen um 20 Prozent gesenkten Energieverbrauch als Ziel. Richtlinien und rechtliche Regelungen werden verschärft. Gerade im Baugewerbe sind Energieeinsparungen von bis zu 65 Prozent gefordert. Durch umweltfreundlichere Heiz- und Kühlsysteme sowie Ressourcen sparende Baumaterialien sollen die Kosten erheblich minimiert werden. Ein Viertel des Gebäudebestandes soll mit energiesparenden Maßnahmen saniert werden.[29] Noch ist man diesen hochgesteckten Zielen in keiner Weise näher gekommen. Um sie zu erreichen, werden erfahrene Architekten aus dem Ausland eingeladen, neuartige »moderne« Ökokonzepte umzusetzen.
Bereits seit 2002 verwendet AS&P für die Häuser in der neuen Stadt Anting Wärmedämmung, weil dies auch Bestandteil einer »guten deutschen Stadt« ist. Im Wohnprojekt MOMA Beijing setzte das Österreicher Architekturbüro Baumschlager & Eberle aktuelle Gebäudeklimakonzepte wie Betonkernkühlung und kontrollierte Wohnraumbelüftung um, die einen Standard erreichen, der sogar europäische Normen übertrifft.[30]
Die Planung des Hypergreen-Tower in Shanghai von Jacques Ferrier in Kooperation mit der Lafarge-Gruppe sieht vor, dass 70 Prozent des eigenen Energiebedarfs durch Geothermik, zehn Windkraftanlagen und 3.000 Quadratmeter Photovoltaikpaneele selbst erzeugt werden. Kontrollierte Wohnraumbelüftung, natürliche Ventilation und die zweischalige Fassade senken den Energiebedarf zusätzlich.[31]
Ähnliches wird am Pearl River Tower des amerikanischen Büros SOM in Guangzhou umgesetzt. Nach seiner Fertigstellung im Jahr 2009 wird er

[25] *Linie 4, 5, 10, Airport Line und Olympic Line.*
[26] *Zu großen Teilen durch »Renovierung« (Abriss) ehemaliger Dörfer. Vgl. Barbara Münch, Michael Arri: Simultane Realitäten – Urban Villages in Chinas expandierenden Metropolen, in: Gregor Jansen: totalstadt.beijing case. High Speed Urbanisierung in China, Köln 2006, S. 188-195.*
[27] *Ungefähr die Größe der Stadt Kassel.*
[28] *Vgl. auch Agnès Sinai: Spätes Erwachen im Treibhaus China, in: Le Monde Diplomatique 1/2007.*
[29] *Energieeffizienz, ein Leitmotiv für den 11. Fünfjahresplan, in: Infobrief China 2006 (www.china.ahk.de).*
[30] *www.minergie.ch/download/Referat_Eberle.pdf*
[31] *www.lafarge.com*

wohl der erste Null-Energie-Wolkenkratzer der Welt sein. Über die bewährten Klima- und Energiekonzepte hinaus[32] lenkt eine speziell geformte Fassade die Windströmungen an der Hochhausscheibe in zwei Windkanäle, wo sie durch Turbinen in Energie umgewandelt werden. Brennstoffzellen, Luftfeuchtenkondensatoren und Wärmetauscher runden das Klimakonzept ab und dienen zusätzlich der Frischwassergewinnung.[33]
Ein wichtiger Aspekt dieser Projekte ist, dass ihnen die ökologischen Eigenschaften deutlich angesehen werden. In China wird keine Lehmhütte zurückhaltend in zweiter Reihe gebaut. Es müssen auffällige Großprojekte sein, die die ganze Welt zum Staunen bringen.

China ist aufgrund des Wirtschaftswachstums, fehlender Umweltschutzauflagen und ökologisch fataler Projekte wie dem weltweit kritisierten Drei-Schluchten-Staudamm auf dem Weg, der größte Umweltsünder der Welt zu werden. Andererseits werden gleichzeitig radikale Ökologiekonzepte in Dimensionen realisiert, wie sie sonst nirgendwo möglich sind. Doch bei allen Anstrengungen Chinas, sich als Land der ökologischen Superlative zu profilieren, erscheinen solche Vorzeigeprojekte angesichts des verheerenden Raubbaus an Natur und Gesundheit der Menschen als fragwürdige Imagepflege.

CHINAS JUNGE ARCHITEKTEN

Wichtiger Bestandteil der aktuellen Architekturszene ist eine nicht mehr unbedeutende nationale Avantgarde-Bewegung. Die sehr häufig imagebeladene, rücksichtslose und plakative Herangehensweise der jüngeren Vergangenheit hat eine Gegenströmung erzeugt, die weit entfernt vom Mainstream europäischen Vorbilds gute Architektur produziert.
Eine junge Generation von chinesischen Architekten, die meist im Ausland studiert haben, kehrt nach China zurück und entwirft Gebäude in eigenen Büros, unabhängig von großen Designinstituten. Funktionalität und ein sehr subtiler Umgang mit regionalen Eigenheiten zeichnet diese Architektur aus. Durch geschicktes und pragmatisches Taktieren mit Zwängen werden Konzepte mit größerem Bewusstsein für Materialität, Raum, Landschaft und soziale Strukturen entwickelt. So werden Bestandsgebäude miteinbezogen, regionale Technologien und Raumkonzepte angewandt, lokale Materialien verwendet und mit einer zeitgenössischen Architektursprache verbunden.
Die Gegenbewegung ist nicht auf die drei Metropolen Shanghai, Beijing und Hongkong beschränkt. Es ist eine Architektur der Nische. Kleinere Projekte mit viel Spielraum stehen im Vordergrund. Dort, wo selbstbestimmt gehandelt werden kann, ohne dass große nationale Interessen erfüllt werden müssen, sind diese Architekten erfolgreich. Bauherren sind die sich neu bildenden gehobenen Eliten mit ihren individuellen Bedürfnissen. Sie geben kleinen Ateliers ohne »First Class«-Registrierung[34] die Möglichkeit, eigene klare Gestaltungsideen zu entwickeln und umzusetzen, ohne ihre Gebäude mit allzu vielen Bedeutungen überfrachten zu müssen. Entgegen

[32] Doppelschalige Fassade, Sonnenschutzglas und Verschattung, Betonkernkühlung und Photovoltaik.

[33] Zentralverband Sanitär Heizung Klima (Hg.): Energie und Architektur, Berlin 2007.

[34] Um öffentliche Aufträge zu bekommen oder um Ausführungsplanung und Baubegleitung zu betreiben, ist eine »First Class«-Registrierung erforderlich. Im Zuge der Privatisierung des Planungswesens in den Neunzigerjahren wurde dieses System eingeführt. Auch wenn die Zahl der Registrierungen ansteigt, ist es immer noch schwierig, diese Lizenz zu bekommen. Vgl. Eduard Kögel: Zur Lage junger Architekten in China, in: archplus, Heft 168, S. 71ff.

der üblichen Praxis werden Bauvorhaben von Anfang bis Ende begleitet, so dass die Ideen auch wirklich und mit Qualität umgesetzt werden.
Die Wegbereiter der Avantgarde Ma Qingyun, LIU Jiakun, Ai Wei Wie, Zhang Lei und Wang Shu haben in kleinen Büros angefangen, Villen, Privathäuser sowie auch Restaurants und Läden mit hoher Entwurfs- und Ausführungsqualität umzusetzen.[35] So hat beispielsweise Ma Qingyun nach seinem Auslandsaufenthalt mit dem Haus für seinen Vater in Lantian seine selbstständige Bautätigkeit in China begonnen. Ai Wei Wei errichtete als erstes Architekturprojekt in einer 60-Tage-Performance sein eigenes Heim. Villen für Künstler folgten.
Eines der herausragendsten und ungewöhnlichsten Projekte der neuen Avantgarde ist das kleine Liuyeyuan-Museum für buddhistische Skulpturen von LIU Jiakun (Atelier Feichang). Ein privater Bauherr gab es in Xinmin, einem kleinen Dorf in der Nähe von Chengdu, in Auftrag. Trotz der Besinnung auf lokale Bautechniken und Materialien wie Beton setzt sich das Gebäude durch seine archaische Architektursprache von der trivialen Umgebung ab. Auf einem Steg, der über einen im Bambushain gelegenen Lotusteich hinwegführt, gelangt der Besucher durch eine kleine Öffnung in das Innere des künstlichen Steins. Die ausgeklügelte Wegführung wird dort fortgesetzt, lenkt den Besucher an den Ausstellungsstücken entlang und ermöglicht immer wieder fokussierte Blicke in die Landschaft und den Innenraum. Dabei wird sowohl dem Element Wasser wie auch der traditionellen Architektur jeweils die Bedeutung zurückgegeben.

Seit ein paar Jahren versuchen neben privaten Bauherren auch Universitäten, durch anspruchsvollere Architektur ihr Image auf einer qualitativ hochwertigen Ebene in Szene zu setzen. Notwendig ist eine Architektursprache, die international besonders wegen eines konzeptionellen Ansatzes und einer klar strukturierten Umsetzung Anerkennung findet.
Eines der ersten Vorzeigeprojekte dieser Art ist die Bibliothek des Wenzheng College, Suzhou von Amateur Architecture Studio (Wang Shu): eine Kreuzung aus chinesischer Pavillonarchitektur und Weißer Moderne. Entstanden ist ein Gebäude mit übereinander gestapelten, zweigeschossigen Lesesälen, die über große Glasflächen zum Wasser orientiert sind. Ein Mittelteil mit Eingangsbereich durchstößt den Hauptbau und gibt einen losgelösten, sich dem Wasser annähernden Lesepavillon frei. Die simple Form und eine logische Gliederung unterstützen die Klarheit und Deutlichkeit der Architektursprache.
In ähnlich durchdachter Weise haben auch MADA s.p.a.m. den Campus der Zhejiang Universität in Ningbo, Zhang Lei die Gebäude der Nanjing-Universität sowie das Atelier Deshaus den Campus des Institute of Technology in Dongguan neu gestaltet.[36] Das Atelier Z+ (Zhang Bin, Zhou Wei) schafft mit dem neuen Gebäude der Architekturfakultät der Tongji-Universität in Shanghai die Grundlage für eine gute Ausbildung neuer Architekten. Jeden Monat entstehen neue Büros mit selbstbewussten, markigen und mehrdeu-

[35] *Vgl. Eduard Kögel: Made in China. Neue chinesische Architektur, München 2005.*
[36] *Institut für Elektrotechnik, Institut für Freie Künste und Institut für Computerwissenschaften.*

tigen Namen wie Urbanus, Standardarchitecture oder Atelier 100s+1, die auf ähnliche Weise versuchen, gute Architektur zu produzieren.
Die Wegbereiter der neuen Architektur sind inzwischen weltbekannt, auf internationalen Ausstellungen vertreten und bekommen große Aufträge, die bis vor Kurzem noch ausschließlich an etablierte Designinstitute oder internationale Architekturbüros vergeben wurden. Das Büro MADA s.p.a.m. (Ma Qingyun) realisierte beispielsweise neben Projekten in Wuxi, Longyang, Xian und Qingpu gleich mehrere Großvorhaben in Ningbo. Der Tianyi-Platz gibt der Stadt ein neues Zentrum und schafft dabei einen öffentlichen Raum mit hoher Aufenthaltsqualität, wie es ihn in China bisher nicht gegeben hat. Zudem versuchten die Architekten mit diesem Projekt, die Kleinteiligkeit der historischen Stadt mit der Maßstäblichkeit einer neu erwachsenden Metropole zu verbinden. Das Wohn-, Gewerbe- und Entertainmentviertel »Y-Town« nördlich vom Zentrum Ningbos verbindet in einem ehemaligem Hafengebiet historische Bausubstanz mit einer neuen Architektur, die sich an die traditionellen Formen anlehnt, punktuell aber durch gezielt gesetzte Solitäre den Gegensatz zur historischen Bausubstanz kontrastiert. Einer dieser modernen Bauten ist das Museum für Stadtplanung. Räume von unterschiedlicher Nutzung und Größe beeinflussen subtil die Fassadenstruktur aus verschiedenfarbigen Glasbausteinen, so dass sich innere Strukturen auch an der Außenhaut andeuten.[37]

Bei fast allen Projekten der neuen Generation sind die Einflüsse aktueller westlicher Architektur unverkennbar. Zwar arbeiten hier chinesische Architekten, diese haben jedoch oft im Ausland studiert und eine westlich geprägte Herangehensweise mitgebracht. Zurück in ihrer Heimat, versuchen sie diese Erfahrungen mit chinesischer Tradition und Baukultur zu verbinden, entfernen sich dabei aber zunehmend von dem, was die meisten ihrer Landsleute als »chinesisch« empfinden. In den diagrammatisch-abstrakten Herangehensweisen und sich überlagernden Schichten von MADA s.p.a.m. ist die langjährige Zusammenarbeit mit Rem Koolhaas spürbar. Der Umgang mit Materialien bei LIU Jiakun hat eine materialistische Herangehensweise, wie man sie sonst eher aus der Schweiz kennt. Zugegeben, die Arbeit der jungen »Unabhängigen« leitet einen Qualitätssprung ein, den man der Architektur in China gewünscht hat. Aber die hochwertigen Sichtbetonwände knüpfen so abstrakt an chinesische Baukultur an, dass sie in vordergründiger Deutlichkeit zunächst eine maximale Distanz evozieren. Und so wie in Europa die Moderne der Zwanzigerjahre noch ein avantgardistisches Einzelleben geführt hatte, besteht auch hier die Gefahr, dass diese Form der Architektur ein Einzelphänomen bleibt, das in der großen Masse der trivialen imagebeladenen Allerweltsarchitektur untergeht.

EXPERIMENTELLER PRAGMATISMUS

Der große Teil der gebauten Architektur kombiniert unter Missachtung von Konzept und Bedeutung alles irgendwie mit allem. Bis auf wenige Ausnah-

[37] *Vgl. Kristin Feireiss, Hans Jürgen Commerell: Ningbo. Metamorphose einer chinesischen Stadt, Berlin 2003.*

men ergibt sich eine gleichförmig aufregende und ekklektisch-symbolisch überfrachtete Architektur. Nicht ohne Reiz, gleichwohl ohne jeden innovativen Wert. Kopiert werden darf alles, was erfolgreich ist. Chinesische Architektur ist inzwischen so umfangreich publiziert und der Pool an eigenen Bauwerken so groß, dass nicht mehr nur auf europäische Architektur zurückgegriffen werden muss. Weniger fremde, sondern zunehmend eigene erfolgreiche Konzepte bilden immer öfter wichtige Bezugspunkte. So ist zum Beispiel das Dach der Oper von Shanghai ein äußerst beliebtes Motiv, das oft reproduziert wird. Und auch das Projekt »The New Bund« in Shanghai-Pudong ahmt die erfolgreiche Uferbebauung der Metropole nochmals nach.

Besonders im Wohnungsbau wurde der gezielte Symbolismus inzwischen durch puren Pragmatismus ersetzt. In reinen Schlafstädten mit wenig Service, ohne Arbeit und ohne Leben stehen Hochhäuser mit 200 Metern Höhe versetzt zueinander, nach Süden hin gestaffelt, nach Norden gestaucht. Die Südseite gehört Balkonen und Wohnzimmerfenstern – konzipiert nach Computerprogrammen, die den Sonnenstand für jedes Zimmer der eigenen sowie der Nachbarbebauung berechnen.[38] Grundrisse werden immer wieder verwendet, Variationen gibt es nur bei der Auswahl der Farbe und in ein paar Fassadendetails: Hauptsache, dem Sockel fehlt nicht das Vordach und dem Penthouse nicht die Antenne. Durch opulente Schmuckelemente, Rahmen und Kronen täuschen die großen Gebäude üppigere Raumprogramme vor als tatsächlich vorhanden sind. Vielfältige Formen bilden bloß ein zusammengewürfeltes Agglomerat aus Massen. Gebaut wird, was im Rendering wirksam ist: große Flugdächer, Wasserläufe mit Springbrunnen, knallige und glänzende Fassaden.

Das Problem der Monotonie, typisch für die Neunzigerjahre, ist durch den freien Immobilienmarkt[39] endgültig beseitigt. Überwunden ist auch das Einerlei weiß gefliester Häuserreihen mit grün gefärbter Verglasung. Die verschiedenen Auffassungen über den richtigen Stil führen zu unterschiedlichsten Gebäuden. So wechseln sich neue Hochhäuser mit blauer, grüner oder gelber Fassade mit wiederhergestellten Tempeln und Stadtvillen im europäischen Stil ab: ein Nebeneinander von traditioneller und moderner Architektur.

Wenn es möglich ist, bleibt die Architektur trotzdem kontextbezogen. In einen Park mit eingebundener Pavillonarchitektur werden keine Wolkenkratzer platziert. Ebenso wird in einem New Business District keine Tempelarchitektur gebaut, wenn sie nicht schon vorhanden war. Eine Ferienanlage wird bevorzugt im spanischen Stil errichtet, weil es dem gängigen Image von Urlaub entspricht, und die Ausstellungshallen der Terrakotta-Armee prangen geradezu zwangsläufig im monumentalen Stil. Zu einem Bahnhof gehört eine moderne Stahl-Glas-Konstruktion (Beispiel: Bahnhof Suzhou), es sei denn, er fungiert als Tor zu einer historisch bedeutenden Stadt (wie zum Beispiel der Bahnhof Kaifeng).

[38] *Die Vorschrift, dass in jede Wohnung mindestens eine Stunde lang die Sonne scheinen muss, ist gleichzeitig das wichtigste Verkaufsargument. Manchmal liegt der Verdacht nahe, dass bestimmte Gestaltungsabsichten, wie große Öffnungen in der Fassade, ausschließlich auf solche Regeln zurückzuführen sind.*

[39] *Vgl. Eduard Kögel: Die letzten hundert Jahre: Architektur in China, in: Gregor Jansen: totalstadt.beijing case. High Speed Urbanisierung in China, Köln 2006, S. 99-123.*

Die verwendeten Zeichen richten sich nach dem gewünschten Ausdruck: entweder Modernität oder Traditionsbewusstsein beziehungsweise westlich oder chinesisch. So sucht sich eine Gesellschaft im Zangengriff zwischen Tradition und Moderne eine ihr gemäße Architektur. Die Vielfalt der Stile und Zeichen ist Ausdruck einer sich differenzierenden Gesellschaft, die eine geschlossene kollektive Identität zugunsten einer Pluralität von Bewusstseins- und Identifikationslagen aufgegeben hat.

AUSBLICK

Dass die kritische chinesische Architektur inzwischen weltweit wahrgenommen wird und in Ausstellungen in Berlin,[40] Rotterdam,[41] Paris[42] und Venedig[43] gezeigt wird, gibt Anlass zu Optimismus. Denn diese Position festigt ihr Gewicht im Heimatland. Die Protagonisten der Anfänge der Avantgardebewegung sind mittlerweile Professoren an den Universitäten und bilden eine neue Architektengeneration aus.[44] Zunehmend sehen Bauherren und Entwickler ein, dass sie mit konzeptionell durchdachten und qualitativ hochwertigen Objekten sowie ökologischen Strategien einen Wettbewerbsvorteil erzielen können. Der Mut, mit erfinderischen Experimenten zu anderen Lösungen zu kommen, ist ohne Zweifel gewachsen.
China bietet auf dem Gebiet der Architektur die Möglichkeit, unter Ausnutzung aller Potenziale weltweit einzigartige Lösungen zu finden. Grundstückseigentum spielt noch immer eine untergeordnete Rolle, so dass Planungen in ungeahnten Größenordnungen denk- und realisierbar sind. Das Tempo bei der Verwirklichung ist ebenso beispiellos wie die Lust auf Experimente. Die weitere Öffnung des Landes schafft mehr Freiraum für private Initiativen. Ungebrochener Know-How-Transfer führt zur Verbesserung der Qualität. Mit einem sich verschärfenden Stadt-Land-Gegensatz sowie absehbaren demographischen Konflikten stehen der Architektur und dem Städtebau Chinas große Aufgaben bevor.
Unter diesen Bedingungen ist die junge Architektengeneration mit ihrem besseren Verständnis für Konzept und Kontext gut gerüstet. Ob ihr auf der Weltbaustelle China tatsächlich die Zukunft gehört, bleibt abzuwarten.

[40] *Aedes Berlin: TU MU. Junge Architektur in China, 21. September bis 28. Oktober 2001; Aedes Berlin: MADA On Site, 06. Februar – 21. März 2004 (ebenso in Barcelona, Wien und Birmingham).*
[41] *NAI Rotterdam: China Contemporary, 10. Juni bis 03. September 2006.*
[42] *Centre Pompidou: What about China?, 25. Juni bis 13. Oktober 2003.*
[43] *Beitrag des Künstlers und Architekten Chang Yung Ho auf der Biennale in Venedig 2005.*
[44] *Chang Yung Ho ist Dekan am Graduate Center for Architecture an der Universität Beijing. Anfang 2007 hat Ma Qingyun einen Posten als Dekan der School of Architecture an der University of Southern California (USC) angetreten. Wang Lu ist Professor an der Tsinghua-Universität in Beijing und Chefredakteur der Zeitschrift »World Architecture Magazine«.*

IMPRESSUM

IMPRINT

The *Deutsche Bibliothek* lists this publication in the *Deutsche Nationalbibliografie*; detailed bibliographic data is available on the internet *http://dnb.ddb.de*.

Die *Deutsche Bibliothek* verzeichnet diese Publikation in der *Deutschen Nationalbibliografie*. Detaillierte bibliografische Daten sind im Internet über *http://dnb.ddb.de* abrufbar.

ISBN 978-3-938666-30-2

www.dom-publishers.com

Texte Cornelia Dörries, Berlin (Architektenporträts), Christian Dubrau, Berlin (Einleitung) | **Lektorat** Uta Keil, Berlin
Übersetzung Cord von der Lühe, Berlin | **Grafische Gestaltung** Susanne Weigelt, Leipzig | **Druck** Shenzhen